Troubled Partnership

U.S.-Turkish Relations in an Era of Global Geopolitical Change

F. Stephen Larrabee

Prepared for the United States Air Force

PROJECT AIR FORCE

The research described in this report was sponsored by the United States Air Force under Contract FA7014-06-C-0001. Further information may be obtained from the Strategic Planning Division, Directorate of Plans, Hq USAF.

Library of Congress Cataloging-in-Publication Data

Larrabee, F. Stephen.
    Troubled partnership : U.S.–Turkish relations in an era of global geopolitical change / F. Stephen Larrabee.
      p. cm.
    Includes bibliographical references.
    ISBN 978-0-8330-4756-4 (pbk. : alk. paper)
    1. United States—Foreign relations—Turkey. 2. Turkey—Foreign relations—United States. 3. National security—United States. 4. National security—Turkey. 5. United States—Military relations—Turkey. 6. Turkey—Military relations—United States. 7. World politics—1989– 8. Geopolitics. 9. Social change. I. Title.

E183.8.T8L36 2010
327.730561—dc22

                2009042096

Cover image courtesy of AP Photo/Charles Dharapak.

Published 2010 by the RAND Corporation
1776 Main Street, P.O. Box 2138, Santa Monica, CA 90407-2138
1200 South Hayes Street, Arlington, VA 22202-5050
4570 Fifth Avenue, Suite 600, Pittsburgh, PA 15213-2665
RAND URL: http://www.rand.org/
To order RAND documents or to obtain additional information, contact
Distribution Services: Telephone: (310) 451-7002;
Fax: (310) 451-6915; Email: order@rand.org

Preface

With the end of the Cold War, many Turks feared that Turkey would lose its strategic significance in American eyes. These fears, however, have proven to be unfounded. Rather than decreasing, Turkey's strategic significance has increased. Turkey stands at the nexus of four geographic areas of growing strategic importance in the post–Cold War era: the Balkans, the Middle East, the Caucasus/Central Asia, and the Persian Gulf region. In each of these areas, Turkey's cooperation is critical for achieving U.S. policy goals.

However, in recent years—especially since 2003—U.S.-Turkish relations have undergone serious strains. Sharp differences over Iraq and the Kurdish issue have been compounded by differences over the Middle East, particularly relations with Iran, Iraq, and Syria. At the same time, Turkey has witnessed a sharp rise in anti-American sentiment.[1] This monograph examines the causes of recent strains in the U.S.-Turkish security partnership and options for reducing these strains. It should be of interest to U.S. policymakers and other U.S. officials monitoring developments in Turkey and its neighborhood.

This research was sponsored by the Director of Operational Planning, Policy and Strategy, Regional Issues Directorate, Office of the Deputy Chief of Staff, Operations, Plans and Requirements, Headquarters United States Air Force (AF/A5XX), and was conducted within the Strategy and Doctrine Program of RAND Project AIR FORCE as part

---

[1] See Transatlantic Trends, *Transatlantic Trends: Key Findings 2007*, Washington, D.C.: German Marshall Fund of the United States, 2007, p. 21. See also Pew Global Attitudes Project, *Global Unease with Major Powers*, Pew Research Center, June 27, 2007.

of a fiscal year 2007 study entitled "Troubled Partnerships: The Growing Challenge of Managing U.S. Security Relationships and Implications for the United States Air Force."

RAND Project AIR FORCE

RAND Project AIR FORCE (PAF), a division of the RAND Corporation, is the U.S. Air Force's federally funded research and development center for studies and analyses. PAF provides the Air Force with independent analyses of policy alternatives affecting the development, employment, combat readiness, and support of current and future aerospace forces. Research is conducted in four programs: Aerospace Force Development; Manpower, Personnel, and Training; Resource Management; and Strategy and Doctrine.

Additional information about PAF is available on our Web site: http://www.rand.org/paf/

Contents

Figures

Summary

A strong security partnership with Turkey has been an important element of U.S. policy in the Mediterranean and the Middle East since the early 1950s. It is even more important today. Turkey stands at the nexus of four areas that have become increasingly critical to U.S. security since the end of the Cold War: the Balkans, the Middle East, the Caucasus/Central Asia, and the Persian Gulf region. In all four areas, Turkey's cooperation is vital for achieving U.S. policy goals.

However, in the last few years—and especially since 2003—U.S.-Turkish relations have seriously deteriorated. The origins of many of the strains can be traced back to the first Gulf War. However, the strains were significantly exacerbated by the fallout from the 2003 U.S. invasion of Iraq, which resulted in a serious deterioration in Turkey's security environment. As a consequence of the invasion, sectarian violence in Iraq increased, and the Iraqi Kurds' drive for autonomy and eventual independence gained greater momentum. (See pp. 11–20.)

Turkish officials fear that the creation of a Kurdish state on Turkey's southern border could intensify separatist pressures in Turkey and pose a threat to its territorial integrity. These fears have been exacerbated by the resumption of an insurgency by the Kurdistan Workers' Party (PKK), which has stepped up cross-border terrorist attacks against Turkish territory from sanctuaries in northern Iraq. These terrorist attacks are Turkey's number-one security concern. (See pp. 25–29.)

The U.S. reluctance to take military action against the PKK or to allow Turkey to take unilateral military action against PKK sanctuaries in northern Iraq after the 2003 invasion caused serious strains in

Washington's relations with Ankara. It also provoked a sharp rise in anti-American sentiment in Turkey, which, if not halted, threatens to pose serious long-term consequences for the U.S. security partnership with Turkey.

These strains have been compounded—and to some extent reinforced—by differences over policy toward Iran and Syria. Whereas the United States sought until very recently to isolate both countries, Turkey has pursued a policy of rapprochement with Iran and Syria. As a result, U.S. and Turkish policies toward Iran and Syria have been increasingly at odds. This divergence began to manifest itself before the assumption of power in Ankara by the Justice and Development Party in 2002, but it has become more pronounced since then. (See pp. 34–40.)

Iran's nuclear ambitions could become a further source of strain. Turkey is concerned by Iran's nuclear program because such a program could stimulate a regional arms race, which could force Turkey to take compensatory measures. However, Turkey is strongly opposed to a military strike against Iran, fearing that a strike would lead to further destabilization of the Middle East. A U.S. military strike against Iran would create a crisis in U.S.-Turkish relations and could prompt the Erdoğan government to halt or curtail U.S. use of Turkish military facilities, particularly the air base at İncirlik. (See pp. 36–37.)

U.S. defense cooperation with Turkey has undergone a downturn in the last few years. Congress has held up a number of major weapon sales to Turkey due to Turkey's human-rights policy and policy toward Cyprus. Turkey has begun to regard the United States as a less-than-reliable defense partner and has expanded its defense relationships with countries that impose fewer procurement restrictions, particularly Israel and Russia. The U.S.-Turkish defense-industry relationship has stagnated lately. Until Sikorsky finalized a sale of 17 Seahawk helicopters in fall 2006, no U.S. firm had won a major direct commercial sale in Turkey since 2002. (See pp. 77–87.)

Revitalizing U.S.-Turkish Relations: The Policy Agenda

The arrival of a new administration in Washington presents an important opportunity for repairing the fissures in the U.S.-Turkish security partnership and putting relations on a firmer footing. President Barack Obama's visit to Ankara in April 2009 helped to set a new tone in relations. But the visit needs to be followed up by concrete steps in a number of areas outlined below if the U.S.-Turkish security partnership is to be infused with new vitality and strength.

Northern Iraq and the PKK

The United States should increase its political and intelligence support for Turkey's struggle against PKK terrorism. U.S. support for Turkey's struggle against the PKK is regarded by Turkish officials as the litmus test of the value of the U.S.-Turkish security partnership. The visible increase in anti-American sentiment in Turkey in recent years has been driven to an important degree by a perception that the United States is tacitly supporting the Iraqi Kurds. Strong support for Turkey's struggle against the PKK would have an important political-psychological impact on Turkish public opinion and help undermine this widespread perception. (See pp. 119–120.)

In addition, the United States should put greater pressure on the Kurdistan Regional Government (KRG) to crack down on the PKK and cease its logistical and political support of the group. Such pressure would have a positive impact on Washington's relations with Ankara and weaken the growth of anti-American sentiment among the Turkish public. However, anti-American sentiment in Turkey has complex roots and reflects more than just discontent with President George W. Bush's policy toward Iraq and the PKK. Thus, any shift in U.S. policy is likely to take longer to have a positive impact on public attitudes in Turkey than elsewhere in Europe. (See p. 120.)

The PKK threat cannot be resolved by military means. A strong antiterrorist program is essential, but to be successful, it must be combined with social and economic reforms that address

the root causes of the Kurdish grievances. The Erdoğan government's "Kurdish Opening," launched in the summer of 2009, represents an encouraging sign that the government is beginning to recognize this. The initiative has sparked an intense internal debate in Turkey. If the initiative proves to be a serious effort to address Kurdish grievances, it could significantly reduce tensions between the Turkish authorities and the Kurdish community in Turkey and contribute to the wider process of democratization in the country. (See p. 120.)

The United States should strongly encourage and support Turkey's efforts to open a direct dialogue with the leadership of the KRG in northern Iraq. There can be no stability on Turkey's southern border over the long term without an accommodation between the Turkish government and the KRG. This does not mean that Turkey should recognize an independent Kurdish state, but for regional stability to exist, Turkey needs to work out a modus vivendi with the KRG. Ultimately, this can only be achieved through a direct dialogue with the KRG leadership. The Erdoğan government has taken important steps in this direction since late 2008. Indeed, the two sides appear to be moving by fits and starts toward a rapprochement. However, the rapprochement is fragile and needs strong U.S. support. (See pp. 120–121.)

As the United States withdraws its forces from Iraq, it needs to intensify efforts to defuse tension between the KRG and the central government in Baghdad. This growing tension represents a serious threat to Iraq's viability as an integral state and could seriously complicate Turkey's security challenges. The U.S. military presence has acted as an important stabilizing force in northern Iraq and helped prevent tension between the Iraqi Kurds and Arabs from breaking out into open conflict. But U.S. leverage and ability to influence the situation on the ground in Iraq will decline as the United States draws down its military forces. Thus, the United States needs to intensify efforts to get the two sides to resolve their political differences—especially their boundary disputes—*now* while Washington still has some political leverage. The United States should maintain some military presence in northern Iraq as long as possible without violating the terms of the Status of Forces Agreement signed with the Maliki government at the end of 2008. This could help prevent current tension from escalating into open conflict as the two sides seek to resolve their political differences. (See p. 121.)

The Middle East

U.S. policymakers should avoid portraying Turkey as a model for the Middle East. The notion of Turkey as a model makes many Turks, especially the secularists and the military, uncomfortable because they feel it pushes Turkey politically closer to the Middle East and weakens Turkey's Western identity. In addition, they fear that it will strengthen political Islam in Turkey and erode the principle of secularism over the long run. The latter concerns are particularly strong within the Turkish armed forces. (See p. 121.)

The United States should continue to express a readiness to open a dialogue with Iran and Syria and to engage both countries in diplomatic efforts to help stabilize Iraq as it draws down its forces there. Such a move is unlikely to lead to dramatic changes in Iranian or Syrian policy overnight, but it would make it harder for the two regimes to blame the United States for the poor state of bilateral relations and could open new possibilities for enhancing regional stability over the longer run. At the same time, it would bring U.S. and Turkish policy into closer alignment and reduce an important source of friction in U.S.-Turkish relations. (See pp. 121–122.)

Washington should also intensify its efforts to persuade Tehran to abandon any attempt to acquire nuclear weapons. A nuclear-armed Iran would have a destabilizing impact on security in the Persian Gulf region and could spark a nuclear arms race in the Gulf and Middle East, a race that could have important consequences for Turkish security. To date, Turkey has shown little interest in developing its own nuclear deterrent, and it is unlikely to do so as long as the U.S. nuclear guarantee and the North Atlantic Treaty Organization (NATO) remain credible. However, if Turkish relations with Washington and NATO deteriorate, Ankara might be prompted to consider acquiring a nuclear deterrent of its own. This underscores the importance of maintaining close U.S.-Turkish security ties and keeping Turkey firmly anchored in NATO. (See p. 122.)

Eurasia and the Caucasus

The United States should support recent efforts to promote an improvement in relations between Turkey and Armenia, particularly the opening of the Turkish-Armenian border. The normalization of relations between Ankara and Yerevan would significantly contribute to enhancing peace and stability in the Caucasus. It would also enable Armenia to reduce its economic and political dependence on Russia and Iran. Thus, a normalization of relations between Turkey and Armenia is strongly in U.S. interests. (See p. 122.)

The Obama administration should work closely with Congress to prevent the passage of an Armenian genocide resolution. Passage of such a resolution could cause the Erdoğan government to come under strong domestic pressure to take retaliatory action against the United States, possibly curtailing U.S. use of İncirlik Air Base. Such a move would have a strongly detrimental impact on the ability of the United States to resupply its forces in Afghanistan and could complicate the withdrawal of U.S. combat troops from Iraq. At the same time, Turkey should be encouraged to address more openly the events surrounding the mass deaths of Armenians at the hands of the Ottoman authorities in the final days of the Ottoman Empire. Clarification of the events during this tragic period is a prerequisite for a durable and lasting reconciliation with Armenia and would enhance Turkey's reputation as an open and modern democratic state. (See pp. 122–123.)

Turkish Membership in the European Union

The United States should continue to support Turkey's membership in the European Union (EU). Turkey's integration into the EU would strengthen the EU and help put to rest the claim that the West—especially Europe—is innately hostile to Muslims. This could have a salutary effect on the West's relations with the Muslim world. Indeed, a moderate, democratic Turkey could act as an important bridge to the Middle East. Conversely, rejection of Turkey's candidacy could provoke an anti-Western backlash, strengthening the forces in Turkey that want to weaken Turkey's ties to the West. Such a development is in the interest of neither the EU nor the United States. (See p. 123.)

However, given the sensitivity of the issue of Turkey's EU membership among EU member states, the United States should support Turkish membership through quiet diplomacy behind the scenes and avoid overt pressure and arm-twisting. Such tactics are likely to cause resentment among EU members and could even hurt Turkey's chance of obtaining membership. At the same time, Washington needs to recognize that Turkish membership in the EU—if it occurs—would alter the tone and character of U.S.-Turkish relations over the long run. Although Ankara will continue to want strong security ties to Washington, Turkish leaders would look increasingly to Brussels rather than to Washington on many issues once Turkey joined the EU. As a result, Turkey's foreign policy would likely become more "Europeanized" over time. (See pp. 123–124.)

Turkish-Greek Relations and Cyprus

The United States should intensify efforts to get Greece and Turkey to resolve their differences over the Aegean. Although Turkish-Greek relations have significantly improved since 1999, differences over the Aegean continue to mar bilateral relations and pose a threat to stability in the Eastern Mediterranean. Unless these differences are resolved, there is a danger that some incident could escalate out of control and lead to armed conflict, as almost happened over the islets of Imia/Kardak in February 1996. At a time when NATO faces serious challenges in Afghanistan and the post-Soviet space, the last thing the United States needs is a new crisis in the Aegean. (See p. 124.)

The United States should also encourage and support the intensification of the intercommunal dialogue being conducted under UN auspices between the two Cypriot communities. Although the danger of Turkish-Greek conflict over Cyprus has receded in recent years, the lack of a Cyprus settlement remains an important obstacle to Turkey's aspirations for EU membership. Progress toward a settlement of the Cyprus dispute would give Turkey's membership bid critical new momentum at a time when accession negotiations have visibly slowed. It would also contribute to greater overall security and stability in the Eastern Mediterranean. (See p. 124.)

Defense Cooperation

In the wake of the Obama visit, Washington should initiate a broad strategic dialogue with Ankara about the future use of Turkish bases, particularly İncirlik. Given Turkey's growing interests and increasingly active policy in the Middle East, Ankara is likely to be highly sensitive about allowing the United States to use Turkish bases, especially İncirlik, for Middle East contingencies. The United States therefore cannot assume that it will have automatic use of Turkish bases in Middle East contingencies unless such use is regarded as being in Turkey's direct national interest. (See pp. 124–125.)

Ballistic missile defense could be an important area for future U.S.-Turkish defense cooperation. In light of the growing threat posed by the possible acquisition of nuclear weapons by Iran, the United States should explore missile-defense options, both bilaterally and through NATO, to ensure that Turkish territory is protected against the growing threat posed from ballistic missiles launched from the Middle East. (See p. 125.)

Democratization and Domestic Reform

The United States should encourage Turkey to undertake further steps to revitalize the process of democratization and domestic reform. Although the Erdoğan government pursued a reformist agenda during its first several years, the process of democratization and domestic reform has slowed since 2005 and needs new impetus. These reforms are necessary not only to give Turkey's EU-membership bid new traction—they are also important in their own right independent of Turkey's desire to gain admittance to the EU. (See p. 125.)

The United States should not overreact to the growth of religious consciousness in Turkey. Turkish Islam is more moderate and pluralistic than Islam elsewhere in the Middle East. Turkey's long history of seeking to fuse Islam and Western influences dates back to the late Ottoman period. This history differentiates Turkey from other Muslim countries in the Middle East and enhances the chances that Turkey will be able to avoid the sharp dichotomies, ruptures, and violence that have characterized the process of political modernization in the Middle East. Moreover, the more democracy, pluralism, and tolerance there is in Turkey, the less threatening the growth of religious consciousness will be. (See pp. 125–126.)

Acknowledgments

The author would like to express his appreciation to Marc Grossman, Ian Lesser, and Barak Salmoni for their helpful comments on an earlier draft of this monograph. He would also like to thank Morton Abramowitz, Mustafa Akyol, Egemen Bağış, Gen Edip Başer, Mehmet Ali Birand, Matt Bryza, Cengiz Çandar, Ahmet Davutoğlu, Dan Fata, Emre Gönensay, Richard Holbrooke, Robert Hunter, Yusuf Kanlı, Suat Kınıklıoğlu, Aliza Markus, David Ochmanek, Soli Özel, Mark Parris, Gen (ret.) Joseph Ralston, Defne Samyeli, Özdem Sanberk, Nabi Şensoy, Gönül Tol, İlter Turan, Ross Wilson, and Yaşar Yakış for their helpful insights during preparation of the manuscript. Any mistakes or errors of judgment are solely the responsibility of the author.

Abbreviations

AKP	Justice and Development Party
bcm	billion cubic meters
Blackseafor	Black Sea Naval Cooperation Task Force
CENTCOM	U.S. Central Command
CHP	Republican People's Party
DTP	Democratic Society Party
EC	European Community
EU	European Union
GCC	Gulf Cooperation Council
KRG	Kurdistan Regional Government
MOU	memorandum of understanding
NATO	North Atlantic Treaty Organization
NSC	National Security Council
PAF	Project AIR FORCE
PKK	Kurdistan Workers' Party
PUK	Patriotic Union of Kurdistan
TESEV	Turkish Economic and Social Studies Foundation
TGS	Turkish General Staff
TRNC	Turkish Republic of Northern Cyprus
UN	United Nations

Introduction

Since joining the North Atlantic Treaty Organization (NATO) in 1952, Turkey has been an important U.S. strategic ally. During the Cold War, Turkey served as a critical bulwark against the expansion of Soviet military power into the Mediterranean and the Middle East. Ankara tied down 24 Soviet divisions that otherwise could have been deployed against NATO on the Central Front in Europe. It also supplied important facilities for monitoring and verifying U.S. arms-control agreements with the Soviet Union.

With the end of the Cold War, many Turks feared that Turkey would lose its strategic significance in American eyes. These fears, however, have proven to be unfounded. Rather than decreasing, Turkey's strategic significance has increased. Turkey stands at the nexus of four geographic areas of growing strategic importance in the post–Cold War era: the Balkans, the Middle East, the Caucasus/Central Asia, and the Persian Gulf region. In each of these areas, Turkey's cooperation is critical for achieving U.S. policy goals.

However, in recent years—especially since 2003—U.S.-Turkish relations have undergone serious strains. Sharp differences over Iraq and the Kurdish issue have been compounded by differences over the Middle East, particularly relations with Iran and Syria. At the same time, Turkey has witnessed a sharp rise in anti-American sentiment.[1]

---

[1] See Transatlantic Trends, *Transatlantic Trends: Key Findings 2007*, Washington, D.C.: German Marshall Fund of the United States, 2007, p. 21. See also Pew Global Attitudes Project, *Global Unease with Major Powers*, Pew Research Center, June 27, 2007, p. 3.

This has led some observers to suggest that in the next few years, the United States could witness a new debate on "Who lost Turkey?"[2]

This monograph explores the sources of these strains and their implications for U.S.-Turkish relations. Chapter Two focuses on changes in Turkey's security environment and their impact on U.S.-Turkish security ties. Chapters Three and Four examine the effects of the U.S. invasion of Iraq and of Turkey's relations with the Middle East, while Chapter Five focuses on Turkey's interests in Russia and Eurasia. Chapter Six looks at the recent difficulties in Turkey's relations with Europe, while Chapter Seven examines recent trends in U.S.-Turkish defense cooperation. Chapter Eight examines focuses on domestic changes in Turkey and their implications for Ankara's future foreign-policy orientation. Chapter Nine identifies alternative ways in which Turkey could evolve in the next several decades and examines their potential implications for U.S. policy. The monograph's conclusion, Chapter Ten, identifies concrete steps that the United States could take to revitalize the U.S.-Turkish security partnership.

---

[2] See Philip Gordon and Ömer Taşpınar, "Turkey on the Brink," *Washington Quarterly*, Vol. 29, No. 3, Summer 2006, pp. 57–70.

CHAPTER TWO

The U.S.-Turkish Security Partnership in Transition

Turkey and the United States have been close security partners for more than half a century. Their partnership was forged in the early days of the Cold War and shaped by the Soviet threat. Stalin's territorial demands after World War II—including demands for a base on the Straits and border adjustments at Turkey's expense—were the driving force behind the establishment of a U.S. security partnership with Turkey.

The enunciation of the Truman Doctrine on March 12, 1947, led to the expansion of U.S. defense ties to Turkey and laid the ground-work for Turkey's eventual incorporation into NATO in 1952.[1] During the Cold War, Turkey served as an important barrier to the expansion of Soviet power into the Mediterranean and the Middle East. Ankara also provided important installations for monitoring and verifying Moscow's compliance with arms-control agreements.

U.S. and Turkish Interests

The end of the Cold War eliminated the original impetus for the U.S.-Turkish security partnership, but it has not diminished Turkey's

---

[1] The primary motivation for the enunciation of the Truman Doctrine was the commu-nist threat to Greece. Aid to Turkey was a secondary consideration. As one witness testified before the House Committee on Foreign Affairs, "Turkey was slipped into the oven with Greece because that seemed to be the surest way to cook a tough bird." See George S. Harris, *Troubled Alliance: Turkish-American Problems in Historical Perspective, 1945–1971*, Washing-ton, D.C.: American Enterprise Institute for Public Policy Research, 1972, p. 28.

strategic importance—as many Turks initially feared—in American eyes. On the contrary, Turkey's strategic importance has increased, not decreased, since the fall of the Berlin Wall. However, the rationale for the security partnership has significantly changed. Today, Turkey's strategic importance to the United States lies not in deterring a threat from Russia but rather in its capacity to provide a bridge to the Muslim world and serve as a stabilizing force in the Middle East and the Caucasus/Central Asia—two areas of increasing strategic importance to the United States.

Continued access to Turkish bases, especially the air base at İncirlik, remains important for achieving U.S. interests in the Greater Middle East. Over 70 percent of U.S. military cargo sent to Iraq is flown through İncirlik Air Base or is sent by land through Turkey.[2] If the Turks were to curtail or refuse U.S. access to Turkish facilities, particularly İncirlik, this would have a serious impact on the ability of the United States to supply its forces in Afghanistan. Such actions could also complicate the withdrawal of U.S. combat forces from Iraq.

The security relationship remains important for Turkey as well. Turkey lives in a tough and volatile neighborhood and has disputes with several neighbors (i.e., Syria, Iraq, Greece, and Armenia). It also is within range of missiles fired from Iran and Iraq. Thus, Turkey views its security relationship with the United States as an important insurance policy against its growing exposure to risks coming from the Middle East. Although U.S. involvement in the Middle East also entails risks for Turkey, on balance, Turkey benefits from the U.S. military presence in adjacent regions.

The United States is also Turkey's most important arms supplier. Despite recent efforts at diversification, Turkey still conducts roughly 80 percent of its defense-industrial activity with the United States. Large numbers of Turkish officers have been trained in the United States.[3] This has allowed the Turkish armed forces to develop close ties

---

[2]   See, for instance, David Cloud, "U.S. Seeks Alternatives If Turkey Cuts Off Access," *New York Times*, October 11, 2007.

[3]   Turkey has been the highest-funded International Military Education and Training program since 9/11; indeed, such funding to Turkey has doubled since 2001 (information provided to the author by Department of Defense officials, April 30, 2009).

to their American counterparts and obtain a deeper knowledge of U.S. military operational doctrine and thinking.

Finally, the United States has strongly supported important Turkish strategic priorities outside the defense realm. For example, it has been a stalwart advocate of the construction of the Baku-Ceyhan oil pipeline, which is designed to bring Caspian oil to world markets via a terminal on Turkey's Mediterranean coast. The United States has also strongly backed Turkey's bid for European Union (EU) membership and supported Turkey's struggle against the Kurdistan Workers' Party (PKK) separatists much more vigorously than have Turkey's European allies.

Changing Turkish Perceptions of the Security Partnership

Despite the end of the Cold War, Turkey has powerful reasons for wanting to maintain close security links to the United States. However, Turkish perceptions of the benefits of ties to the United States have shifted markedly in the last several decades. During the Cold War, the feeling that Turkey derived important benefits from its security relationship with the United States was widespread among the Turkish elite and general population alike.

This perception began to change after the Cyprus crisis in 1963–1964. The famous "Johnson letter"—in which President Lyndon Johnson warned that the United States might not come to Turkey's defense if Turkish intervention in Cyprus provoked a Soviet response—came as a shock to the Turks. The crisis underscored that there were costs associated with being so heavily dependent on the United States, and it prompted an effort by Ankara to broaden its security ties and reduce its dependence on Washington.

The perception that there were important costs attached to maintaining close security ties to the United States was reinforced in 1975, when the United States imposed an arms embargo on Turkey in response to the Turkish invasion of Cyprus. The embargo was regarded by Turkey as a slap in the face to a loyal ally and led to a sharp deterioration of U.S.-Turkish relations. It is still remembered with bitterness today, coloring Turkish attitudes about the degree to which the United States can be considered a reliable ally.

These crises put severe strains on the U.S.-Turkish partnership and prompted Turkey to begin to diversify its foreign policy and reduce its dependence on the United States for its security. However, this effort to diversify its foreign policy was mitigated by the constraints imposed by the Cold War. Faced with a residual Soviet threat, both sides felt the need to maintain a strong security partnership.

Since 1990, however, Turkey's security environment has undergone an important shift prompted by three major developments: (1) the collapse of the Soviet Union and the end of the Cold War, (2) the 1990–1991 Gulf War, and (3) the 2003 U.S. invasion of Iraq. These three factors have had a profound effect on Turkish security perceptions—and on the solidity and strength of the U.S.-Turkish security partnership.

The End of the Cold War

The disappearance of the Soviet threat removed the main rationale behind the U.S.-Turkish security partnership and reduced Ankara's dependence on Washington for its security. At the same time, it opened up new opportunities and vistas in areas that had previously been neglected or were off-limits to Turkish policy, particularly the Middle East and the Caucasus/Central Asia. No longer a flank state, Turkey found itself at the crossroads of a new strategic landscape that included areas where it had long-standing interests, historical ties, or both. Ankara sought to exploit this new diplomatic flexibility and room for maneuver by establishing new relationships in these areas.

In addition, with the end of the Cold War, the locus of threats and challenges to Turkish security shifted. During the Cold War, the main threat to Turkish security came from the north—from the Soviet Union. Today, Turkey faces a much more diverse set of security threats and challenges: rising Kurdish nationalism and separatism; sectarian violence in Iraq, which could spill over and draw in outside powers; the possible emergence of a nuclear-armed Iran on Turkey's doorstep; and a weak, fragmented Lebanon dominated by radical groups with close ties to Iran and Syria. Most of these threats and challenges are on or close to Turkey's southern border.

As a result, Turkish strategic attention is today focused much more on the Middle East than it had been in the past because this is where the key threats and challenges to Turkish security are located. At the same time, the shift in the locus of threats and challenges southward has given Turkey a stronger interest in maintaining both stability on its southern border and cordial ties to its regional neighbors, particularly Iran and Syria—two countries with which the United States has serious differences. As a result, U.S. and Turkish interests in and policies toward both countries—and the Middle East more broadly—have increasingly diverged in recent years.[4]

The Impact of the Gulf War

The 1990–1991 Gulf War had a profound impact on Turkish security and Turkish security perceptions. Although many American officials tend to regard the war as a kind of "golden age" of U.S.-Turkish cooperation, the Turkish perception is quite different. For many Turks, as Ian Lesser has noted, the Gulf War is "where the trouble started."[5]

President Turgut Özal saw the war as an opportunity to demonstrate Turkey's continued strategic importance and cement closer defense ties to the United States. He hoped that his firm support of the U.S. military campaign against Iraq would bring important foreign-policy dividends in terms of strengthening the "strategic partnership" with the United States and enhancing Turkey's prospects for achieving membership in the European Community (EC), as the EU was then called.

However, Özal's expectations went unfulfilled. The strategic partnership with the United States never materialized. Özal's support of

---

[4] See F. Stephen Larrabee, "Turkey Rediscovers the Middle East," *Foreign Affairs*, Vol. 86, No. 4, July/August 2007, pp. 103–114.

[5] See Ian O. Lesser, "Turkey, the United States, and the Geopolitics of Delusion," *Survival*, Vol. 48, No. 3, Autumn 2006, p. 2.

the United States also did little to advance Turkey's membership in the EC. Economically, Turkey paid a high price for its support of the U.S. military campaign in terms of pipeline fees and lost trade. Financial losses incurred and the lack of tangible benefits accruing from Turkish support of the United States in the Gulf War contributed to a growing perception in Ankara that Turkey gets much less from the relationship than does the United States.

In addition, the war marked a major escalation of Turkey's Kurdish problem. The establishment of a de facto Kurdish state in northern Iraq under Western protection gave new impetus to Kurdish nationalism and provided a logistical base for attacks on Turkish territory by Kurdish separatists in the PKK. In fact, many Turks viewed U.S. support for the Kurdish entity in northern Iraq as part of a conscious plan to support the emergence of an independent Kurdish state on Turkey's southern border.

Finally, the Gulf War reinforced Turkish sensitivities regarding national sovereignty. Özal's willingness to allow the United States to use Turkish facilities to conduct sorties against Iraq during the war has been the exception, not the rule. Generally speaking, the Turks have been very wary of allowing the United States to use their facilities for non-NATO contingencies. For example, Turkey refused to allow the United States to launch offensive strikes against Baghdad, including during both the 1996 crisis over Iraqi operations in the north and Operation Desert Fox.

The United States, the United Kingdom, and France were allowed to monitor the no-fly zone over northern Iraq after the conclusion of the Gulf War, but the U.S. use of İncirlik Air Base to patrol the no-fly zone was unpopular among many Turkish officials and military leaders. The Turkish government imposed significant constraints on U.S. freedom of action, and the agreement to use the bases had to be renewed every six months, causing frequent delays and strains in U.S.-Turkish relations. Many Turkish officials and parliamentarians feared that U.S. actions could exacerbate Turkey's security problems with its neighbors, and the Pentagon resented the frequent efforts by the Turks to restrict U.S. freedom of action.

The overall impact of the Gulf War was to heighten U.S.-Turkish discord. On the one hand, the Turks felt they had not been sufficiently compensated for either the support they had given the United States or the economic losses they had incurred as a result of that support. On the other hand, the war exacerbated the security challenges on Turkey's southern border, especially the Kurdish problem, which Turkish officials regarded as an existential threat to the territorial integrity of the Turkish state.

CHAPTER THREE

Iraq and the Kurdish Challenge

Many of the current problems in U.S.-Turkish relations are a direct outgrowth of the U.S. decision to invade Iraq. The invasion exacerbated many of the latent strains and tensions that had been bubbling beneath the surface since the end of the Cold War and gave them new impetus. At the same time, it brought the differing regional security perceptions and interests of both sides into sharper conflict. The U.S. action strongly conflicted with the Justice and Development Party's (AKP's) efforts to reduce tensions with Turkey's immediate neighbors.

Turkish leaders had strong reservations about the U.S. invasion from the outset. They had no love for Saddam Hussein, whom they regarded as a brutal dictator. However, Saddam provided stability on Turkey's southern border. For Ankara, this was the paramount consideration. Turkish officials feared that Saddam's overthrow would lead to an increase in sectarian violence, the strengthening of Kurdish nationalism, and the fragmentation of Iraq as an integral state, thereby exacerbating Turkey's security dilemmas.

In addition, public opinion in Turkey was overwhelmingly opposed to the invasion. According to opinion polls, close to 90 percent of the Turkish population opposed the invasion. Opposition was particularly strong among supporters of the ruling AKP, which had strong Islamic roots. The party had assumed power only a few months before the invasion and was not prepared to face a crisis of such seriousness in its early months in office.

The March 1, 2003, Parliamentary Vote

The refusal of the Turkish Grand National Assembly on March 1, 2003, to allow the United States to use Turkish territory to open a second front against Iraq should be seen against this broader background. This refusal came as a shock to U.S. officials, who had expected the resolution to pass since the AKP had a strong majority in the parliament, and dealt a serious political blow to relations between Ankara and Washington. Many U.S. officials saw the vote as a lack of solidarity on Turkey's part and a betrayal of a loyal ally.

In reality, the vote was the result of miscalculations and mistakes on both sides. The Turks overestimated Turkey's leverage and bargaining power. Convinced that the United States could not launch an invasion of Iraq without using Turkish territory, they made excessive demands, both economic and political, that U.S. officials ultimately rejected as unacceptable. In the end, U.S. officials concluded that the price for Turkish cooperation was simply too high. Rather than continuing to haggle with the Turks and risking further delays that could jeopardize the invasion, President George W. Bush and his advisers decided to proceed with the invasion without opening a second front from Turkish territory.

However, the United States also bears some responsibility for the outcome. The United States had used Turkish bases to launch sorties against Iraq during the Gulf War and to patrol the no-fly zone in northern Iraq, but it had never before asked Ankara to allow U.S. ground forces to be deployed on Turkish soil in order to launch an invasion of one of its Turkey's neighbors. This part of the U.S. request thus significantly raised the bar and put the new AKP government, which had been in office only a few months, under extreme pressure to accede to an action that was opposed by the overwhelming portion of the Turkish population, especially its own political base, and that threatened to have major consequences for Turkish security.

Some U.S. officials, especially Secretary of State Colin Powell, thought the United States might be asking too much of the Turks and expressed strong reservations about asking for Turkey's approval to use Turkish territory to open the second front. The Turks, Powell suggested, could probably accept overflight rights. But he was skeptical about their willingness to agree to the movement of large numbers of land forces, especially heavy armored or mechanized divisions, across Anatolia to invade another Muslim country. As he put it, that "may be too many bricks on the scale for the Turks. I don't think we can get it, and we are taking a risk at losing it all by going for that."[1]

Powell's concerns proved to be highly accurate. However, they were largely ignored. U.S. officials were convinced that at the end of the day, the Turkish military, which traditionally exerted a decisive influence on important national security decisions, would ensure that the bill passed. However, the Turkish General Staff (TGS), the bastion of Turkish secularism, did not trust the AKP because of the party's Islamic roots. It wanted the AKP leadership to have to take full responsibility for the decision, which the military knew would be unpopular with the party's base as well as with the Turkish population more broadly. The TGS therefore did not actively lobby for passage of the bill, assuming that it would still pass, since the AKP had an overwhelming majority in the Grand National Assembly. To the TGS's surprise—and to that of most U.S. officials as well—the bill failed to pass by three votes.

The Grand National Assembly's action greatly tarnished Ankara's image in Washington as a reliable ally and dealt a severe blow to U.S.-Turkish relations. Many U.S. officials regarded the Turkish action as an unwarranted act of betrayal by the Turks. The vote left a sour aftertaste that burdened relations for several years thereafter. At the same time, the negative vote deprived Turkey of any means of influencing the occupation and post-conflict reconstruction of Iraq.

Mutual trust and confidence were further undermined by several incidents shortly after the fall of Baghdad. The most serious incident occurred in Al-Suleymaniyah in northern Iraq on July 4, 2003, when U.S. forces, acting on an intelligence tip, arrested and hooded a group of Turkish Special Forces officers who were allegedly planning to assassinate the mayor of Kirkuk. Although the Turkish soldiers were released a few days later, the spectacle of U.S. forces humiliating hooded and

---

[1] Bob Woodward, *Plan of Attack*, New York: Simon & Schuster, 2004, p. 325.

shackled Turkish soldiers caused a furor in Turkey and greatly contributed to a further souring of bilateral relations.[2]

The Resurgence of the PKK

Turkey was one of the biggest losers of the U.S. invasion of Iraq. The invasion had four important consequences for Turkish security—all of them negative. First, in Iraq, the invasion led to an increase in sectarian violence and the fragmentation of the central government's control over the country. Second, the invasion resulted in an increase of Iranian influence both in Iraq and in the region more broadly. Third, and most important from the Turkish point of view, as a result of the invasion, the Iraqi Kurds' drive for autonomy—and eventual independence—gained greater momentum. Turkish officials feared that the creation of a Kurdish state on Turkey's southern border could exacerbate separatist pressures in the county and pose a threat to its territorial integrity.[3]

Fourth, in the aftermath of the invasion, Turkey was confronted with an upsurge of violence perpetrated by the PKK. The PKK insurgency has resulted in the death of more than 35,000 Turks and Kurds since 1984.[4] After the capture of PKK leader Abdullah Öcalan in 1999,

---

[2] The exact circumstances surrounding the Al-Suleymaniyah incident remain murky. Much of the problem seems to have been the result of poor communication between U.S. and Turkish forces. Although the United States took most of the blame for the incident—at least in Turkish eyes—the Turks appear to have been pursuing their own agenda and acting without consulting U.S. commanders regarding their plans. For a detailed discussion of the incident that does a good job of trying to sort fact from fiction, see James E. Kapsis, "From Desert Storm to Metal Storm: How Iraq Has Spoiled U.S.-Turkish Relations," *Current History*, November 2005, pp. 380–389.

[3] These fears, although deeply held by many Turks, may be exaggerated. According to a survey conducted by MetroPOLL, an independent center that carries out strategic and social studies, in 14 cities in southeastern Turkey, where the majority of people are of Kurdish origin, only 1 percent of respondents would prefer to live in northern Iraq if an independent Kurdish state were established there. See Göksel Bozkurt, "Kurdish Hopes in Turkish State," *Turkish Daily News* (Istanbul), November 12, 2007.

[4] On the origins, rise, and changing goals of the PKK, see Aliza Marcus, "Turkey's PKK: Rise, Fall, and Rise Again?" *World Policy Journal*, Vol. 24, No. 1, Spring 2007b, pp. 75–84.

the PKK declared a unilateral ceasefire, and the violence temporarily subsided. However, the PKK took up arms again in June 2004 and has since launched repeated attacks on Turkish territory from sanctuaries in the Kandil Mountains in northern Iraq. These attacks have resulted in the death of several hundred Turkish security personnel.

As the PKK attacks increased, the Erdoğan government came under growing domestic pressure to take military action to halt the PKK threat, and it repeatedly requested U.S. military assistance to help eliminate PKK training camps in northern Iraq. However, Washington was reluctant to take military action against the PKK because an assault against the PKK would have diverted troops needed to combat the insurgency in Baghdad and other parts of Iraq. U.S. officials also feared that military action against the PKK would destabilize northern Iraq, which was relatively calm compared to the rest of Iraq. The Iraqi Kurds were the staunchest backers of U.S. policy in Iraq, and U.S. administration officials regarded Kurdish support as essential to maintaining a unified Iraq.

Policy differences within the U.S. government also hindered the implementation of an effective and coherent U.S. policy toward the PKK. U.S. Central Command (CENTCOM), which had overall military responsibility for the Iraq mission, placed primary emphasis on fighting the insurgency in central Iraq, and it regarded Turkey's concern about the PKK as a sideshow and distraction from its primary mission. By contrast, both U.S. European Command, which had military responsibility for Turkey, and the Bureau of European and Canadian Affairs in the State Department were more sympathetic to Turkish concerns.

As a result of these internal differences, Turkey's requests for military assistance against the PKK never really got serious high-level policy attention for a long time. Although the United States expressed strong verbal support for Turkey's struggle against the PKK, Washington was unwilling to provide Ankara with concrete military assistance against the PKK. It also opposed any cross-border military attacks by Ankara

---

See also Henri J. Barkey and Graham E. Fuller, *Turkey's Kurdish Question*, Lanham, Md.: Rowman & Littlefield Publishers, 1998.

against PKK training camps and sanctuaries in northern Iraq, fearing that this could destabilize the Kurdish-dominated areas in northern Iraq, which were relatively stable in comparison with the rest of Iraq.

Growing Anti-American Sentiment

The reluctance of the United States to take direct military action against the PKK or to allow Turkey to do so was deeply resented in Ankara and contributed to a dramatic growth of anti-American sentiment in Turkey. According to a survey undertaken by the Pew Charitable Trust in 2007, fewer than one in ten Turks (9 percent) held a positive opinion of the United States—a drop of 21 points since 2002.[5] According to the same survey, 83 percent of respondents said their attitude toward the United States was unfavorable, including 75 percent who felt very unfavorably. This was one of the highest percentages in the Middle East of negative perceptions of the United States, second only to the Palestinian public, among whom 86 percent viewed the United States unfavorably.

This sharp increase in anti-American feeling in Turkey has been primarily a reaction to U.S. policy in Iraq, particularly the U.S. reluctance to take military action against the PKK or to allow Turkey to launch military strikes against PKK sanctuaries in northern Iraq. Many Turks saw these refusals as evidence of a double standard and tantamount to tacit U.S. support for the PKK against Turkey. In Turkish eyes, the United States invaded two countries—Afghanistan and Iraq— to eliminate terrorist safe havens, but it refused to help Turkey do the same thing. As the respected Turkish journalist Semih İdiz noted,

> it is very difficult to explain to the Turkish public—especially in an election environment when everyone has been worked up in a way that has not been seen before—why the same U.S. which

---

[5]   See the Pew Global Attitudes Project, 2007. See also the data in Transatlantic Trends, *Transatlantic Trends: Key Findings 2006*, Washington, D.C.: German Marshall Fund of the United States, 2006, pp. 18–19, which reports similar negative Turkish attitudes toward the United States.

crossed an ocean to fight terrorism in Iraq does not help Turkey against the PKK terrorists when Turkish soldiers are being killed daily.[6]

While some analysts have sought to blame the AKP for the growth of anti-Americanism, disenchantment with U.S. policy is widespread and is not limited to any one party. The growth of anti-Americanism is visible across the entire Turkish political spectrum. This is well illustrated by the political evolution of the Republican People's Party (CHP), the main opposition party. Traditionally one of the most pro-Western and pro-American parties in Turkey, the CHP has since 2003 increasingly adopted a more nationalistic and anti-American tone, largely in reaction to U.S. policy in Iraq and to the reluctance of the United States to support Turkey's struggle against the PKK more actively.

Significantly, the change in U.S. policy since late 2007 (discussed in more detail in a later section) has led to only a slight decline in Turkish anti-American sentiment.[7] Turkey remains one of the most anti-American counties in the world. The "Obama bounce," visible elsewhere in Europe, has been considerably weaker in Turkey. This suggests that disenchantment with the United States in Turkey has deep roots and reflects more than simple dissatisfaction with U.S. policy toward Iraq and the PKK. Thus, regaining support for U.S. policy in Turkey is likely to take longer and prove more difficult than elsewhere in Europe.[8]

---

[6] Semih İdiz, "PKK Assures Unsavory Developments for All," *Turkish Daily News* (Istanbul), June 15, 2007a.

[7] See Pew Global Attitudes Project, *Confidence in Obama Lifts U.S. Image Around the World: Most Muslim Publics Not So Easily Moved*, Pew Research Center, July 23, 2009, especially pp. 5 and 17. According to the Pew survey, only 14 percent of the Turks polled viewed U.S. policy favorably—a 2-percent increase over 2008. This was the lowest percentage and the lowest increase in Europe.

[8] There is an important difference between the anti-American feeling in Europe and that in Turkey. In Europe, the anti-American sentiment witnessed after 2003 essentially represented "anti-Bush" feeling and was primarily driven by European opposition to Bush's policies. Thus, when Bush was defeated and President Barack Obama began to espouse policies in tune with European policies—including greater support for climate change, a readiness

The Ralston Mission

The reluctance of the United States to actively assist Turkey in its struggle against the PKK led to growing strains between Washington and Ankara. U.S. officials became particularly concerned in the summer of 2006 when Turkey engaged in a major military buildup along the Turkish-Iraqi border in what appeared to be preparation for a large-scale military incursion into northern Iraq. Although the Bush administration succeeded through intense diplomatic intervention in preventing a Turkish military incursion into northern Iraq, which it feared could lead to a military confrontation between Turkish and Iraqi Kurdish forces and destabilize northern Iraq, the incident drove home the need for Washington to take Turkish concerns about the PKK more seriously.

In August 2006, in an effort to defuse tensions and respond to Turkish concerns about the PKK, the administration appointed Gen Joseph Ralston, former NATO Supreme Allied Commander Europe, as special envoy with responsibility for coordinating policy toward the PKK. Ralston's appointment was initially welcomed in Ankara as a sign that Washington seemed finally to be taking Turkish concerns

---

to open a dialogue with Iran, a stronger adherence to international law, withdrawal of U.S. troops from Iraq, and a greater emphasis on domestic social welfare reforms—anti-American feeling in many countries in Europe visibly declined.

Anti-Americanism in Turkey has deeper and more-complex political and cultural roots than elsewhere in Europe. The United States is seen by many Turks as having a history of opposing Turkish national interests; examples include the two Cyprus crises, the 1975 arms embargo, the economic losses incurred by Turkey during the first Gulf War, and U.S. support for the establishment of an autonomous Kurdish entity in northern Iraq. Thus, the initial U.S. reluctance to assist Turkey against the PKK came against the background of a long list of Turkish grievances at the hands of the United States that dated back some 50 years.

In addition, anti-Americanism in Turkey draws on deep-seated suspicion and mistrust of the West due to the role played by the Western powers in the collapse and dismemberment of the Ottoman empire (the "Sevres Syndrome"). For instance, according to a study by Yilmaz Esmer of Bahçeşehir University in Istanbul, released in 2009, nearly half the Turkish participants polled (47 percent) believe the United States wants to divide Turkey. This different political and cultural context helps explain why Turkish perceptions of U.S. policy are likely to change much more slowly than elsewhere in Europe. For the results of Esmer's study, see "Unneighborliness in Neighborhoods," *Hürriyet Daily News and Economic Review* (Istanbul), June 5, 2009.

about the PKK seriously. However, despite considerable personal effort on Ralston's part, Ralston's mission produced few concrete results, largely because the Bush administration remained divided about decisively supporting Turkey's struggle against the PKK. As a result, the Turks soon became disillusioned with his mission, and the strains in Washington's relations with Ankara deepened.

In the fall of 2007, the PKK stepped up its attacks on Turkish territory. In the wake of these attacks, the government of Recep Tayyip Erdoğan came under increasing domestic pressure, including from the TGS, to take unilateral military action against the PKK. To defuse public pressure and underscore his government's determination to deal forcefully with the PKK, in mid-October 2007, Erdoğan obtained parliamentary approval to conduct a cross-border strikes into northern Iraq. The parliamentary approval strengthened Erdoğan's hand politically both at home and with the United States. At the same time, during a visit to Washington in early November 2007, Erdoğan made a last-ditch effort to obtain U.S. support for a military strike against the PKK.

The Shift in U.S. Policy

Erdoğan's November 5, 2007, visit to Washington marked an important watershed in U.S.-Turkish relations. During the visit, Bush agreed to provide Turkey with "actionable intelligence" against the PKK and reportedly also gave Erdoğan his backing for Turkey to carry out limited surgical strikes against the PKK camps in northern Iraq.[9] Since the visit, cooperation between the U.S. and the Turkish militaries against

---

[9]   Erdoğan's visit was widely viewed in Ankara as a success. In discussions with the Turkish press after the meeting, Erdoğan expressed himself fully satisfied with the results of the meeting. The main Turkish concern going into the meeting was that Turkey would be prevented from taking any military action at all. According to the Turkish press, these fears were not realized. In addition to the U.S. agreement to share actionable intelligence on the PKK with Turkey, Erdoğan reportedly got a green light from Bush for a limited military strike against the PKK that would not target the Kurdish population or risk a hot confrontation between the Turkish military and the Iraqi Kurds. See Mehmet Ali Birand, "Bush Didn't Risk Losing Turkey," *Turkish Daily News* (Istanbul), November 7, 2007. See also Cengiz Çandar, "The Results from the White House; PKK's Elimination Process," *Turkish Daily*

the PKK has markedly improved. Turkey has carried out a number of surgical cross-border strikes against the PKK—reportedly with the aid of U.S. intelligence.[10] The attacks have been aimed at striking PKK camps and units, not attacking the Iraqi Kurdish population or the Kurdistan Regional Government (KRG) leadership. The United States also began to exert stronger pressure on the KRG to crack down on the PKK—another long-standing Turkish request.

The increased U.S. political and military support for Turkey's struggle against the PKK since late 2007 has resulted in an improvement in U.S.-Turkish relations and a slight, though far less visible, decrease in Turkish anti-American sentiment.[11] Cooperation between the U.S. and Turkish militaries in particular has increased. However, the PKK problem cannot be resolved by military means. A tough military stance against PKK terrorism needs to be combined with broad-based social, economic, and legal initiatives by Turkey designed to make the Kurds feel that they enjoy equal rights with the rest of the Turkish population. Without such social, economic, and legal changes, any effort to eliminate the PKK problem is unlikely to be successful—a fact that some Turkish military commanders appear to be beginning to recognize.[12]

News (Istanbul), November 9, 2007b; Semih İdiz, "The Erdogan-Bush Talks: Successful or Not?" *Turkish Daily News* (Istanbul), November 9, 2007b.

[10] Ümit Enginsoy, "US Intel Aid Implied in Strike on PKK," *Turkish Daily News* (Istanbul), December 3, 2007; Ümit Enginsoy and Burak Ege Bekdil, "US Backs Turkey's Anti-PKK Strikes," *Defense News*, December 10, 2007e; Ann Scott Tyson and Robin Wright, "U.S. Helps Turkey Hit Rebel Kurds in Iraq," *Washington Post*, December 18, 2007.

[11] Transatlantic Trends, *Transatlantic Trends: Key Findings 2008*, Washington, D.C.: German Marshall Fund of the United States, 2008, p. 20.

[12] In an interview in November 2007, for instance, General Aytaç Yalman, Commander of the Second Army in 1998, acknowledged that the Turkish military had underestimated the importance of the "social dimension" of the Kurdish conflict—the importance of the Kurdish desire for self-expression in Kurdish and cultural expression. He suggested that if these social aspects had been better understood earlier, the PKK issue would have been easier to resolve and the PKK might not have turned to violence. In addition, General Kenan Evren, Chief of the TGS and later president of Turkey, who led the 1980 military coup, has admitted that, in retrospect, his decision to ban the Kurdish languages appears to have been a mistake that was made on the spur of the moment, without adequate understanding of its long-term political repercussions. These admissions are contained in a series of interviews of leading Turkish military commanders involved in the fight with the PKK. The inter-

Turkish-KRG Relations

The improved atmosphere in U.S.-Turkish relations has been accompanied by important signs of change in Turkey's relations with the KRG. Prior to 2008, the Erdoğan government—and especially the Turkish military—was wary of establishing direct contacts with the KRG authorities, fearing that such contacts would strengthen the KRG's drive for independence. However, since the fall of 2008, the Erdoğan government has begun to intensify contacts with the KRG. In October 2008, Murat Özçelik, Turkey's special envoy to Iraq, and Ahmet Davutoğlu, then Erdoğan's main foreign policy adviser, met with KRG President Massoud Barzani in Baghdad.[13] This was the first high-level contact between Turkish officials and Barzani in four years.

Since then, signs of an emerging rapprochement between Turkey and the KRG have increased.[14] In March 2009, Turkish President Abdullah Gül paid a visit to Baghdad—the first visit to Iraq by a Turkish head of state in 33 years. During his visit, Gül met with KRG Prime Minister Nechiryan Barzani, head of the Kurdistan Democratic Party. This was the first time a Turkish leader had officially met with a high-ranking leader of the KRG.

Gül's visit signified an important evolution in the Turkish approach to dealing with the KRG. During the visit, Gül reportedly used the word *Kurdistan* in referring to the KRG. This represented a significant departure from Turkey's decades-old policy of denying

---

views, conducted by Fikret Bila, a journalist with the Istanbul daily *Milliyet*, provide fascinating insight into the Turkish military's thinking and approach during the 24-year struggle against the PKK. For Yalman's reflections, see "PKK Issue Should Have Been Resolved in Its Social Stage," *Turkish Daily News* (Istanbul), November 12, 2007. For Evren's remarks, see "Banning Kurdish Was a Mistake," *Turkish Daily News* (Istanbul), November 16, 2007.

[13] Sinan Salaheddin, "Turkish Officials Meet Iraqi Kurds in Baghdad," *Boston Globe*, October 15, 2008. See also Gareth Jenkins, "Turkey Bites the Bullet," *Eurasia Daily Monitor*, Vol. 5, No. 196, October 14, 2008b.

[14] See "Outlines of a Kurdish Deal loom in N. Iraq," *Hürriyet Daily News and Economic Review* (Istanbul), March 19, 2009; Charles Recknagel, "Iraq, Turkey Nearing Deal to Deprive PKK of Bases," Radio Free Europe/Radio Liberty, March 24, 2009; Semih İdiz, "A New Era in Turkish Kurdish Ties," *Hürriyet Daily News and Economic Review* (Istanbul), March 20, 2009.

Kurdish identity and the territorial integrity of the KRG. Gül's words caused a major stir in Turkish political circles and represented an important easing of the "Kurdish taboo."[15]

Gül has been one of the strongest advocates of a rapprochement with the KRG and has argued that a "historic opportunity" exists to solve the Kurdish issue.[16] This opportunity has arisen, according to Gül, as a result of the emergence of a "new consensus" within the Turkish leadership and close coordination between the civilian and military authorities. The TGS appears to have dropped its previous objections to a direct dialogue with the KRG authorities, ending—or at least reducing—internal differences within the government that had hindered the pursuit of a coherent policy toward the KRG in the past.

At the same time, there have been signs of a shift in the attitude of the Iraqi Kurds toward the PKK. In response to Gül's call for greater cooperation between Turkey and the KRG, Iraqi President Jalal Talabani, an ethnic Kurd, explicitly called on the PKK to halt its armed struggle, stating that "either they will lay down their arms or they will leave our territory."[17] In addition, during Gül's visit, the two sides discussed ways to expand trade and energy cooperation, including new Turkish investments in the KRG.[18]

Finally, there have been indications within the PKK of a rethinking of the value of armed struggle. In an interview with the respected Turkish journalist Hasan Cemal in May, Murat Karayilan, the PKK's top military leader, expressed hope for a peaceful settlement of the Kurdish issue and stated that if the Erdoğan government would extend the hand of peace, such a gesture would be reciprocated by the PKK.[19]

---

[15] See Şaban Kardaş, "Gul Denies Saying 'Kurdistan' During Iraq Visit," *Eurasia Daily Monitor*, Vol. 6, No. 60, March 30, 2009a.

[16] See Şaban Kardaş, "Opposition Rejects Gul's Call for Consensus on the Kurdish Issue," *Eurasia Daily Monitor*, Vol. 6, No. 96, May 19, 2009c.

[17] Emrullah Uslu, "Gul's Visit to Baghdad: A Sign of Rapprochement with the Kurds?" *Eurasia Daily Monitor*, Vol. 6, No. 56, March 24, 2009a.

[18] Uslu, 2009a.

[19] Emrullah Uslu, "Acting PKK Leader Murat Karayilan Offers Rare Interview to Turkish Press," *Eurasia Daily Monitor*, Vol. 6, No. 88, May 7, 2009c. See also Amberlin Zaman,

Karayilan also stressed that independence was no longer the PKK's goal. This interview seemed to suggest that the PKK leadership—at least important parts of it—had concluded that the Kurdish issue could not be resolved by armed struggle and that the PKK was ready to explore ways of seeking an end to the conflict. To underscore this point, the PKK announced that it would extend the cease-fire, first announced in April 2009, by six weeks (to July 15, 2009).

In short, Turkey and the KRG appear to be edging by fits and starts toward establishing closer ties. Faced with a hostile and powerful Iran with regional ambitions, the growing power of the Shia-dominated central government in Baghdad, and the waning influence of their main patron, the United States, the Iraqi Kurds appear to have concluded that they need to mend fences with Turkey. Any rapprochement with Turkey, however, requires the KRG authorities to crackdown more heavily on the PKK and curtail their cross-border attacks against Turkey. Talabani's statements in the aftermath of Gül's visit to Baghdad suggest that KRG officials may now be ready to take stronger action against the PKK. At the same time, Turkey seems to have come to accept that the PKK problem cannot be resolved without an improvement in its ties to the KRG.

These developments suggest that new prospects may be opening up for defusing the PKK issue and forging closer ties between Ankara and the KRG. A rapprochement between Turkey and the KRG is in the interest of both sides. Turks and Iraqi Kurds share much in common. Both are predominately Sunni, secular, and pro-Western. Neither wants to see an Iraq closely allied with Iran. The economies of the two entities are closely linked and highly interdependent. Approximately 80 percent of the goods sold in the KRG are made in Turkey. Some 1,200 Turkish companies are currently operating in northern Iraq, mostly in construction but also in oil exploration. They have generated over $2 billion in trade and investment and stand to be major beneficiaries of the KRG authorities' plan to launch $100 billion in new infrastructure projects.

"Turkey's Kurds: Toward a Solution," *On Turkey*, German Marshall Fund of the United States, June 4, 2009d.

The KRG's future—particularly its economic future—will depend heavily on its relationship with Turkey. Although the KRG is rich in oil, it needs to be able to extract the oil and transport it to Western markets. Oil pipelines from northern Iraq already flow into Turkish ports on the Mediterranean. They provide the most efficient and cost-effective means to get Iraqi oil to European markets. Thus, both sides have strong incentives to find a political accommodation—what Henri Barkey has termed a "grand bargain"—over the long run.[20]

The Impact of the July 2009 Kurdish Elections

The results of the Kurdish parliamentary and presidential elections in July 2009 could have an important impact on the internal power dynamics in the KRG. The two leading Kurdish parties that have ruled the KRG since the end of the first Gulf War, the Kurdistan Democratic Party, headed by Barzani, and the Patriotic Union of Kurdistan (PUK), led by Talabani, ran on a joint platform, the Kurdistan List, which came in first, winning 57 percent of the vote in the July parliamentary elections.

However, Gorran [Change], a party that is headed by PUK cofounder Nishurwan Mustafa and advocates a reform agenda, did considerably better than expected and came in second, garnering 23 percent of the vote, entitling the party to 25 seats in the 111-person Kurdish parliament. Most of its increased strength came at the expense of the PUK, which has been weakened by internal infighting in recent years. The strong showing by Gorran, especially in Sulaymaniya, the stronghold of the PUK, is likely to affect the internal distribution of power in the KRG, strengthening Barzani's position while weakening that of Talabani. Indeed, the PUK's performance in the elections, together with Talabani's declining health, could spark a struggle for leadership of the PUK.

---

[20] See Henri J. Barkey, "Kurdistandoff," *The National Interest*, July/August 2007a, pp. 51–57.

Barzani was easily reelected as president of the KRG, winning just under 70 percent of the vote. The new Kurdish constitution approved by the Kurdish parliament on June 24, 2009, significantly strengthens the powers of the president at the expense of the parliament. Thus, Barzani has emerged from the elections with a strong mandate, and his political position in the KRG has been strengthened. Barzani is regarded by Turkish officials as more of a Kurdish nationalist than Talabani, and his increased political strength could create some difficulties for Ankara's effort to reach a modus vivendi with the KRG.

The Problem of Kirkuk

Differences over the status of the ancient Ottoman city of Kirkuk in northern Iraq could prove to be a particularly important factor affecting relations between Turkey and the KRG.[21] Kirkuk has a mixed population composed of Kurds, Arabs, and Turkmen, and it sits on top of one of the world's largest oil deposits.[22] The KRG has pursued a conscious policy of "Kurdization" of Kirkuk in the hope of eventually incorporating the city into the territory under its control. Over the past several years, hundreds of thousands of Kurds who were evicted by Saddam Hussein as part of his effort to "Arabize" Kirkuk after the 1974 Kurdish uprising have returned to Kirkuk to reclaim their homes and property, changing the ethnic balance in the city and forcing many Arabs and Turkmen to leave.

The Turks see the process of Kurdization as part of a calculated strategy by the Iraqi Kurds to establish Kurdish control over Kirkuk

---

[21] The Kirkuk problem is extremely complex and cannot be treated in detail here. For a comprehensive and balanced discussion, see International Crisis Group, "Iraq and the Kurds: Resolving the Kirkuk Crisis," *Middle East Report No. 64*, Washington, D.C.: International Crisis Group, April 19, 2007b.

[22] How much oil lies beneath Kirkuk is not clear. The Iraqi Oil Ministry estimates that Kirkuk contains about 15 billion barrels of oil, which is about 16 percent of Iraq's total (and 2 percent of the world's total) proven reserves. Estimates by Western oil firms are lower—between 5.5 billion and 10.0 billion barrels. See Timothy Williams and Suadad Al-Salhy, "Clouds Gathering over Kirkuk," *International Herald Tribune*, May 29, 2009.

and its oil resources. They fear that Kurdish control of the city and its oil wealth would enable the Iraqi Kurds to finance an independent Kurdish state.[23] They want power to be shared among all ethnic groups in the city, not just Kurds—a view supported by the Arab, Turkmen, and other Iraqi minorities living in Kirkuk.

A United Nations (UN) report released in May 2009 outlined several options for treating Kirkuk, including joint Arab and Kurd control of the city. The report was generally viewed favorably by Ankara.[24] However, Turkish, Iraqi, and U.S. officials have expressed concern over the Kurdish parliament's passage of a new draft constitution on June 24, 2009. The constitution lays claim to Kirkuk as well as the disputed provinces of Nineveh and Diyala. If it is ratified in its current form, it could exacerbate ethnic and political tensions between Iraqi Kurds and Arabs as well as spark tensions with Turkey.

The Internal Kurdish Dimension

Relations between Ankara and the KRG in the future will also be significantly influenced by internal developments within Turkey, particularly the Turkish government's willingness to address the grievances of the Kurdish community in Turkey. Since coming to power, the AKP has introduced a number of reforms designed to address these grievances. In August 2002, Kurdish-language broadcasting was introduced on a limited basis. In addition, as part of the same reform program, classes conducted in Kurdish were also approved on a limited basis.

These reforms initially helped the AKP improve its political support among the Kurds, who make up about 20 percent of the Turk-

---

[23] Who will control oil revenues and how those revenues will be distributed remains a subject of considerable controversy. According to an agreement reached in February 2007, Iraqi oil revenues are to be controlled by the Iraqi national government and distributed equally among the Iraqi population. Although large international firms, such as Exxon Mobil, Chevron, and BP, have refrained from signing contracts because of the political and legal uncertainties, a number of smaller firms have rushed to sign production and exploration contracts.

[24] "Turkey OK with UN Report," *Hürriyet Daily News and Economic Review* (Istanbul), May 8, 2009.

ish population. In the July 2007 parliamentary elections, the AKP doubled its vote (from 27 percent in 2002 to 54 percent in 2007) from eastern and southeastern cities that had traditionally voted for pro-Kurdish parties. These increases came at the expense of the Kurdish Democratic Society Party (DTP), which has close contacts with the PKK.

However, the reforms have been introduced in piecemeal fashion, and their implementation has been hindered by bureaucratic obstacles and red tape. It took two years, for example, to make the regulatory changes to allow Kurdish broadcasting by Turkish state-run stations. Private television stations had to wait another two years to get their paperwork approved—and then programming was limited to only 45 minutes per day. Education in Kurdish areas has faced similar delays and obstacles.[25] These delays have served to diminish the political impact of the reforms and bred a certain cynicism among many Kurds about the sincerity of efforts by Turkish state officials to address Kurdish grievances.

Discontent has visibly increased in the Kurdish areas since 2005. During his August 2005 visit to Diyarbakır—the most important Kurdish city in Turkey—Erdoğan was welcomed with open arms by the citizens of the city because of his more-open and more-tolerant approach to Kurdish rights and identity. However, during his visit to the same city in October 2008, Erdoğan faced a massive boycott by the city's citizens. Public transportation was not in operation, and 90 percent of the city's shops were closed to protest his visit. The boycott vividly demonstrated how dramatically the mood in Turkey's Kurdish regions has shifted in the last several years.

The warm welcome given Erdoğan in Diyarbakır in August 2005 reflected Kurdish hopes, based on the more-tolerant attitude evinced by the AKP toward Kurdish concerns and grievances, that a new era was opening in relations between the Turkish authorities and the Kurdish population. However, these hopes have largely been disappointed. In reaction to the stepped-up attacks by the PKK, Erdoğan has increas-

---

[25] Aliza Marcus, *Blood and Belief: The PKK and the Kurdish Fight for Independence*, New York: New York University Press, 2007a, pp. 293–294.

ingly adopted a more nationalistic and statist approach to the Kurdish issue. This shift has helped to reduce strains between the AKP and the military but has exacerbated tensions with the Kurdish population in Turkey.[26]

The growing Kurdish discontent was reflected in the municipal elections at the end of March 2009. The elections represented a clear defeat for the AKP and demonstrated that Kurdish nationalism is on the rise. In the July 2007 elections, the AKP won most of the cities in the predominantly Kurdish southeast. However, in the March 2009 municipal elections, the AKP lost badly in the southeast to the DTP, which campaigned on a platform of Kurdish cultural identity. The AKP's losses were particularly evident in Diyarbakır, where the mayor, Osman Baydemir, a DTP member, was reelected with 65.4 percent of the vote. The AKP candidate, Kutbettin Arzu, won only 31.6 percent. The DTP also won 14 out of 17 districts of Diyarbakır.[27]

The message from the Kurdish regions in the election was loud and clear: Kurdish identity is more important to Turkey's Kurds than any other issue. By distributing such commodities as refrigerators and coal in advance of the election, the AKP tried to woo Kurdish voters by emphasizing its ability to supply goods and services. But this strategy did not work. The Kurds voted overwhelmingly for the DTP, which put its emphasis on Kurdish cultural identity, not material well-being.

The outcome of the municipal elections was a sharp wake-up call for the AKP and made clear that an intensive effort was needed to address Kurdish grievances and concerns. Since the municipal elections, there have been increasing signs that the Erdoğan government intends to launch a comprehensive initiative to address the Kurdish issue. The government has initiated a broad dialogue with many elements of Turkish society, including the major political parties and the

---

[26] Kurds were particularly upset by Erdoğan's speech in Hakkari in early November 2008, when he invoked the statist slogan "one nation, one flag, one motherland and one state" and angrily demanded that "those who oppose this should leave." See "Erdogan in Kreuzfeuer der Kritik," *Neue Zürcher Zeitung*, November 2, 2008.

[27] Mustafa Akyol, "Kurdish Nationalism on the Rise, Ballot Suggests," *Hürriyet Daily News and Economic Review* (Istanbul), May 31, 2009.

military, in an effort to shape the content of the initiative and create public support for it.

The government's Kurdish initiative is an important development. It is the first serious attempt since the Özal period to address the Kurdish issue. If the initiative proves successful, it could have significant consequences for Turkey's political evolution and diminish one of the most serious threats to Turkey's internal stability.[28] It could also give Turkey's EU-membership bid new impetus. However, the initiative faces strong opposition from the nationalist right, especially the Nationalist Action Party and parts of the CHP. Thus, its ultimate impact will depend in large measure on the Erdoğan government's ability to develop a strong political consensus for its initiative.

Turkey's EU-membership aspirations could also become an important factor influencing the Kurdish issue. A poll in 2005 showed that Turkey's Kurds would overwhelmingly prefer to be a part of Europe than part of an isolated "greater Kurdistan."[29] However, since then, Turkey's bid for EU membership has run into an increasing number of obstacles, and domestic support for EU membership in Turkey has declined. If the EU option proves to be a chimera and the Turkish government does not address Kurdish grievances more forthrightly, many Turkish Kurds could begin to look more favorably on a federal solution—or even union with a "greater Kurdistan"—which would significantly complicate both Turkey's internal Kurdish problem and Ankara's relations with the KRG.

---

[28] The Erdoğan government's Kurdish initiative has sparked widespread discussion in the Turkish press and has generated a large variety of views, some of them quite surprising and unorthodox. As İdiz has noted, some of the views expressed openly in the debate would have been unthinkable even five years ago and show how far Turkey has progressed in the last decade in terms of attitudes toward the Kurdish issue and freedom of expression more broadly. See Semih İdiz, "Kurdish Opening Opens Minds," *Hürriyet Daily News and Economic Review* (Istanbul), August 14, 2009b.

[29] *Boston Globe*, January 14, 2007, cited in John Daly, *U.S.-Turkish Relations: A Strategic Relationship Under Stress*, Washington, D.C.: Jamestown Foundation, February 2008, p. 47.

Iraq's Uncertain Political Evolution

One of the most important factors affecting U.S.-Turkish relations in the coming years will be Iraq's political evolution. Although sectarian violence in Iraq has ebbed since mid-2008, a new and potentially more-destructive conflict has emerged as a result of the escalation of tensions and mistrust between the Arabs and the Iraqi Kurds. On several occasions since late 2008, KRG military forces and troops under the command of the central government in Baghdad came close to open military conflict, which was prevented largely by the presence and mediation of U.S. military forces in northern Iraq.[30]

The growing tension is potentially explosive because it intersects with a number of unresolved issues between the KRG and the Maliki government that pose a threat to Iraq's stability. These include differences over the hydrocarbon law and revenue sharing from Iraq's oil reserves; unresolved boundary disputes over some areas in northern Iraq; and differences over the status of Kirkuk and control of the Peshmerga, the Kurdish militia. Efforts to resolve these political issues since late 2008 have largely stalled.[31]

The political stalemate between the two sides has been reinforced by the growing personal animosity between Barzani and Iraqi Prime Minister Nouri al Maliki. The two leaders are barely on speaking terms. As a consequence, working-level committees tasked to deal with important outstanding issues have largely ceased to function, and communication between the two sides has ground to a halt. The situation in Kirkuk remains precarious, and there has been little progress in resolving differences between the KRG and the central government in Baghdad over oil exploration and revenue sharing.

---

[30] One of the most serious incidents occurred on June 28, 2009, when troops loyal to the KRG government faced off with an Arab-led army unit approaching Makhmur, a predominantly Kurdish town situated between Mosul and Kirkuk in northern Iraq. In this case, as in others, a military confrontation was narrowly avoided through active and timely mediation by U.S. military forces stationed in northern Iraq. See Anthony Shadid, "Kurdish Leaders Warn of Strains with Maliki," *New York Times*, July 17, 2009.

[31] For a detailed discussion, see Semih İdiz, "Iraq and the Kurds: Trouble Along the Trigger Line," Middle East Report No. 88, Washington, D.C.: July 8, 2009a.

The U.S. military presence in northern Iraq has acted as an important stabilizing factor and has helped to prevent the disputes between the Iraqi Kurds and the Maliki government from escalating out of control. However, as the U.S. troop withdrawal intensifies, U.S. leverage and ability to influence the situation on the ground in Iraq will inevitably decline, increasing the danger of an outbreak of open fighting between the KRG and the central government in Baghdad.

An outbreak of conflict between the KRG and the central government in Baghdad could lead to increasing domestic pressure for Turkey to intervene, particularly if the outbreak of Kurdish-Arab conflict led to efforts by the KRG to assert control over Kirkuk or resulted in renewed attacks by the PKK against Turkish territory. Faced with a burgeoning conflict with the central government in Baghdad, Barzani would have little incentive—or inclination—to crack down on the PKK. The promising dialogue/détente between Ankara and the KRG could collapse, sharpening the internal polarization in Turkey and prompting calls from nationalist forces in Turkey for Ankara to intervene militarily.

Such a development could put new strains on U.S.-Turkish relations, making any effort to revitalize relations in the short term more difficult. The Obama administration could face strong Turkish pressure to take more-forceful action against the KRG or to slow the withdrawal of U.S. forces from Iraq. In any case, the escalating tensions between the KRG and the central government in Baghdad increase the importance of close consultation and coordination between Washington and Ankara in order to ensure that the interests and policy of both sides are in broad alignment.

The Erdoğan government has offered to allow the United States to use Turkish facilities to withdraw U.S. troops from Iraq.[32] Current U.S. plans call for most U.S. combat troops and equipment to be withdrawn through Kuwait and, possibly, Jordan. However, Turkey could be a useful backup option should unexpected problems or delays in withdrawal through Kuwait and Jordan occur. Whichever route is used to

---

[32] Ümit Enginsoy and Burak Ege Bekdil, "Turkey Agrees to Help U.S. Withdrawal from Iraq," *Defense News*, March 30, 2009a.

withdraw U.S. troops, Ankara is likely to insist on strict procedures to ensure that U.S. equipment left in Iraq does not fall into the hands of the PKK.

CHAPTER FOUR

The Broader Middle East

The last ten years have witnessed a remarkable burst of Turkish activism in the Middle East. After decades of passivity and neglect, Ankara is emerging as an important diplomatic actor in the region. This new activism in the Middle East represents an important departure from 20th-century Turkish foreign policy. Except for a brief period in the 1950s, Turkish foreign policy was characterized by caution and detachment from deep involvement in Middle East affairs. For most of the postwar period, the Middle East was largely off-limits for Turkish foreign policy.

However, Ankara's new activism in the Middle East does not mean that Turkey is about to turn its back on the West. Nor is it a sign of the creeping "Islamization" of Turkish foreign policy, as some critics fear. Rather, as noted in Chapter Two, it represents a response to structural changes in Turkey's security environment since the end of the Cold War. The Middle East is where the most-acute threats and challenges to Turkish security are located. Hence, Turkey has been compelled to give the region increased attention in its foreign policy.

Turkey's greater engagement in the Middle East is part of the broader process of the country's gradual diversification of its foreign policy since the end of the Cold War. In effect, Turkey is rediscovering a region to which it historically has had strong political and cultural ties. Under the Ottomans, Turkey was an active actor—indeed, the dominant power—in the Middle East. The Republican period, during which Turkey essentially turned its back on the Middle East, was an anomaly in Turkish history. Thus, in many ways, Turkey's more active policy in the Middle East of late represents a return to a more traditional pattern of foreign-policy behavior.

U.S.-Turkish Differences over Iran and Syria

Ankara's new activism and deeper involvement in the Middle East have been part of a conscious effort by the Erdoğan government to reduce tensions with Turkey's immediate neighbors, particularly Iran and Syria. However, Turkey's increased engagement with Iran and Syria has clashed with U.S. policy goals and created strains with Washington. In recent years, U.S. and Turkish policies toward Iran and Syria have increasingly diverged. Whereas the United States has sought to isolate Iran and Syria, Ankara has intensified ties to Tehran and Damascus.

The Kurdish issue has been an important driver behind the intensification of Turkey's ties to Iran and Syria. On the Kurdish issue, the interests of the three countries closely overlap. All three countries have substantial Kurdish minorities within their borders, and all three have an interest in preventing the emergence of an independent Kurdish state. This shared interest has provided an important incentive for the growing rapprochement between Ankara and Tehran and Ankara and Damascus.

Turkish cooperation with Iran has intensified, particularly in the security field. During Erdoğan's visit to Tehran in July 2004, Turkey and Iran signed an agreement on security cooperation that branded the PKK a terrorist organization. Since then, the two countries have stepped up cooperation to protect their borders and have increased coordination of intelligence and other activities against the PKK.[1]

Energy has been another important driver behind Turkey's rapprochement with Iran. Iran is the second-largest supplier of natural gas to Turkey, behind Russia. In July 1996, the Erbakan government concluded a $23-billion natural-gas deal with Iran. The deal provided the

---

[1]　However, Iran opposes a major intervention into northern Iraq by Turkish forces, fearing that a Turkish incursion will increase regional instability and could be used to justify U.S. military action. See "Iran Opposes Turkish Incursion into Iraq," *Turkish Daily News* (Istanbul), July 17, 2007.

framework for the long-term delivery of Iranian natural gas to Turkey for the following 25 years. However, the agreement created strains in relations with Washington because it directly undercut U.S. efforts to constrict trade and investment with Iran.

Since 2006, Turkish-Iranian energy ties have continued to expand. In July 2007, Turkey and Iran signed a memorandum of understanding (MOU) to transport 30 billion cubic meters (bcm) of Iranian and Turkmen natural gas to Europe. The deal envisages the construction of two separate pipelines to ship gas from Iranian and Turkmen gas fields. In addition, the state-owned Turkish Petroleum Corporation will be granted licenses to develop three different sections of Iran's South Pars gas field, which has estimated total recoverable reserves of 14 trillion cubic meters.[2]

The United States has strongly criticized the deal.[3] Besides opposing foreign investment in the Iranian gas sector, the United States is also concerned that the deal could undercut U.S.-Turkish cooperation to develop Caspian gas resources and construct a pipeline infrastructure to transport Caspian gas to Turkey and international markets. Instead of pursuing the deal with Iran, U.S. officials want Turkey to intensify cooperation with Azerbaijan to transport gas from the Shah Deniz fields or import gas from Iraq.

However, the Erdoğan government seems determined to go through with the Iranian gas deal. It argues that Turkey needs to diversify its sources of supply in order to avoid becoming too dependent on one supplier. Turkey currently imports over 65 percent of its natural gas from Russia, and Iran represents one of the few alternative suppliers of natural gas that are capable of meeting Turkey's growing energy needs. Although most of the natural gas under the deal with Iran will

---

[2] "Turkey Refuses to Back Down on Iranian Energy Deal," *Eurasia Daily Monitor*, Vol. 4, No. 157, August 13, 2007.

[3] See "US Criticizes Turkey for Iran Energy Deal," *Turkish Daily News* (Istanbul), September 22–23, 2007; "US Uneasy over Turkey Iran Gas Deal," *Turkish Daily News* (Istanbul), July 12, 2007; Ümit Enginsoy and Burak Ege Bekdil, Turkish-Iranian Rapprochement Worries US," *Defense News*, August 6, 2007c; "US Critical of Turkey's Partnership with Iran," *Turkish Daily News* (Istanbul), April 7, 2007.

be exported to Europe, some of it will be used to meet domestic Turkish needs.

In addition, the deal has broader geostrategic benefits. First, it gives Turkmenistan a non-Russian option—which is an important U.S. policy goal. It also keeps alive the EU-sponsored Nabucco pipeline project to transport Caspian gas from Turkey through the Balkans to Austria and Hungary and provides an alternative to the Russian effort to expand its market share of Europe's energy supply. Third, it gives Turkey a chance to become a transit corridor that is outside of the control of the Russian energy conglomerate Gazprom, a move in keeping with the shared U.S. and EU goal of promoting the diversification of Europe's energy supply.

Iran's Nuclear Ambitions

U.S. and Turkish approaches are much more closely aligned when it comes to Iran's acquisition of nuclear weapons. Like the United States, Turkey is opposed to Iran's acquisition of nuclear weapons. Although they do not perceive a serious military threat from Iran, Turkish officials fear that a nuclear-armed Iran could spark a regional arms race and force Turkey to take compensatory measures to ensure its own security. In the short term, Turkish concerns about a nuclear-armed Iran could increase Turkish interest in missile defense.[4]

To date, Turkey has shown little interest in developing its own nuclear deterrent, and it is not likely to do so as long as the U.S. nuclear guarantee and NATO remain credible. However, if relations with Washington and NATO seriously deteriorate, Ankara might be prompted to consider acquiring a nuclear deterrent of its own. The recent decline in Turkish popular support for NATO is therefore reason for concern

---

[4]   In early March 2007, the Turkish Undersecretariat for Defense Industries expressed interest in obtaining antimissile systems to protect critical facilities, particularly from Iranian surface-to-surface missiles. See Ümit Enginsoy and Burak Ege Berdil, "Turkey Modernizes to Face Mid East Threats," *Defense News*, April 23, 2007a.

and could raise the nuclear issue if Turkey comes to feel that it can no longer rely on NATO to ensure its security.[5]

   An escalation of the crisis with Iran over the nuclear issue could exacerbate tensions in U.S.-Turkish relations. Although the Erdoğan government is uneasy about the emergence of a nuclear Iran, it strongly opposes a military strike against Tehran, fearing it would further destabilize the region.[6] If the United States were to undertake military action against Iran, it could not count on the use of Turkish facilities or active Turkish political support for such action. Indeed, a U.S. military strike against Iran could precipitate a serious crisis in U.S.-Turkish relations and prompt Turkey to curtail U.S. access to or use of Turkish military facilities, especially the air base at İncirlik.

The Impact of the June 2009 Iranian Presidential Election

Turkey's growing political and economic ties to Iran give Ankara an understandable desire to see a relaxation of the current tension between Washington and Tehran. Turkey has therefore strongly welcomed the attempt by the Obama administration to open a dialogue with Iran—a move Ankara had long urged. However, the internal turmoil generated by the Iranian presidential election in June 2009 has dimmed the prospects for a significant improvement in U.S.-Iranian relations in the near future.[7]

---

[5]   Turkish support for NATO has declined visibly in recent years. Whereas in 2004, 53 percent of Turks polled by the German Marshall Fund felt NATO was essential to Turkey's security, only 35 percent felt that way in 2007. The 2007 figure represented a 9-percent decrease compared to 2006. See Transatlantic Trends, 2007, p. 22.

[6]   See Ümit Enginsoy and Burak Ege Bekdil, "Turkey Will Not Back U.S. Military Action on Iran," *Defense News*, December 6, 2004.

[7]   The protests and civil unrest in the wake of the Iranian presidential election caught Turkish officials by surprise. Not wanting to risk straining relations with Tehran, Turkish officials adopted a cautious approach and refrained from criticizing the Iranian regime's attempt to repress the large-scale public protests against the manipulation of the election results. Ankara's cautious approach was in marked contrast to the more critical approach adopted by the EU and, to a lesser extent, the United States. For details, see Yigal Schleifer, "Turkey: Iran Upheaval Poses Diplomatic Challenge for Ankara," *Eurasianet*, June 25, 2009.

Despite the Iranian regime's heavy-handed repression of domestic protests questioning the results of the election, Obama has tried to keep the door to a dialogue with Tehran open. However, if Iran rejects his overtures and presses ahead with its nuclear program, Obama will face strong pressure to call for new, tougher sanctions against Iran. This could create new dilemmas for Turkey, both bilaterally and within the context of its membership in the UN Security Council. At a minimum, as Lesser has pointed out, doing business with Tehran will become more difficult and pose more-complex challenges for Ankara.[8]

Iran's political evolution is difficult to predict. However, the political repercussions generated by the election could prove to be more far-reaching than many observers initially anticipated. The protests in the aftermath of the 2009 election have deepened splits in the leadership. It is not just the broad establishment of the Islamic Republic that has split, with reformists and pragmatic conservatives pitted against fundamentalists and the security apparatus. The cohesion of the theocracy has cracked to the point where its core constituents are at odds with each other.[9] If the divisions in the Iranian leadership deepen, Iran could face a period of prolonged domestic turmoil that could force it to turn inward and weaken its ability to pursue an active regional role. This could open new opportunities for Turkey to enhance its regional influence. At the same time, Turkey could find itself under stiff pressure from its Western allies—above all, the United States—to impose sanctions on Iran that could have a negative impact on Ankara's economic ties to Tehran. Thus, Iran could become an important litmus test of Turkey's solidarity with its Western allies.

---

[8]   See Ian O. Lesser, "Russia, Europe, Iran: Three Grand Strategic Issues in U.S.-Turkish Relations," *On Turkey*, German Marshall Fund of the United States, June 19, 2009b, p. 3.

[9]   David Gardner, "Iran's Divided Regime Prevails—at the Cost of Its Legitimacy," *Financial Times* (London), August 8, 2009.

Relations with Syria

Turkey's ties to Syria have also significantly improved of late. Turkish-Syrian relations were seriously strained in the 1980s and early 1990s, particularly because of Syrian support for the PKK. Relations reached a crisis in October 1998 when Turkey threatened to invade Syria if Syria did not cease its support for the PKK.[10] Faced with Turkey's overwhelming military superiority, Syria backed down, expelling PKK leader Abdullah Öcalan and closing PKK training camps on its soil. The expulsion of Öcalan and the closing of the PKK camps opened the way for a gradual improvement in Turkey's relations with Syria, a trend that has gained increased momentum in the last several years.

Turkey's rapprochement with Syria has been driven in particular by a shared concern regarding the threat posed by Kurdish nationalism. Like Turkey, Syria faces an internal problem with its Kurdish minority, which lately has shown increasing signs of restlessness. The Ba'athist leadership around Syrian President Bashar al-Assad is worried that the emergence of an economically robust Kurdish government in northern Iraq could stimulate pressures for economic and political improvements among Syria's Kurdish population and pose a challenge to the regime's stability.

As is the case with Iran, Turkey's closer ties to Syria have created strains with the United States. These strains were particularly visible in the spring of 2005, when U.S. officials sought to persuade Ahmet Necdet Sezer, then president of Turkey, to cancel his visit to Damascus. However, Sezer, with Erdoğan's backing, insisted on making the visit, causing considerable consternation in Washington.

The Obama administration's interest in engaging in a dialogue with Syria could bring U.S. and Turkish approaches toward Syria into closer alignment and decrease the prospect that Syria will be a source of discord in U.S.-Turkish relations. Turkey's good ties to Syria could prove to be an asset in this regard. Turkey played a useful role as a facilitator during talks between Syria and Israel in 2008. However, the

---

[10] For a detailed discussion, see Yuksel Sezgin, "The October 1998 Crisis in Turkish-Syrian Relations: A Prospect Theory Approach," *Turkish Studies*, Vol. 3, No. 2, Autumn 2002, pp. 44–68.

Syrian government has shown little interest in responding positively to Obama's overtures. Syria's continued willingness to allow al Qaeda terrorists and other jihadists to freely cross the Syrian border into Iraq and its efforts to forge closer ties to Iran have dimmed the prospects for an early improvement in U.S.-Syrian relations.

Lebanon and the Broader Regional Stage

Ankara's diplomatic engagement in the Lebanon crisis in the summer and fall of 2006 provides another example of Turkey's new activism in the Middle East. The Erdoğan government's decision to send 1,000 troops to participate in the UN peacekeeping force in Lebanon represented an important departure from Turkey's traditional policy of avoiding deep involvement in Middle Eastern affairs. The decision provoked a lively internal debate in Turkey and was sharply criticized both by Turkey's mainstream parties, whose leaders argued that Turkey should not get actively involved in the conflict, and by some members of Erdoğan's own party, who feared that Turkey could be drawn into a military confrontation with Hizbollah.

The decision provoked an open split between Sezer and Erdoğan. Sezer opposed Turkish participation in the UN peacekeeping force, arguing that it was not Turkey's responsibility to protect others' national interests. Erdoğan, by contrast, maintained that Turkey could not afford to be a mere bystander and that the best way to protect Turkish national interests was to participate in the peacekeeping process. The debate between Sezer and Erdoğan highlighted the difference between the traditional Turkish policy of avoiding involvement in the Middle East and the more activist approach of Erdoğan and then–Foreign Minister Abdullah Gül, who view engagement in the Middle East as essential to shaping developments on Turkey's periphery in directions conducive to Turkish interests.

The decision to participate in the UN peacekeeping mission, though not without risks, had a number of important benefits for Turkey. It allowed Turkey to show that it was a regional player whose influence had to be taken into consideration. It also enabled Turkey to underscore its European credentials by being among the largest European contributors to the UN peacekeeping force in Lebanon. Furthermore, it won accolades in Washington, which had strongly encouraged Turkish participation.

Finally, participation allowed Turkey to demonstrate its newfound commonality of interests with the established Arab states of the region. Relations with Saudi Arabia have been strengthened, as demonstrated by the visit of King Abdullah to Turkey in August 2006—the first visit of its kind in 40 years. Both countries have worked together to try to invigorate the Arab-Israeli peace process and contain Iran's rising power.

Ties to Egypt, another regional power, have also been strengthened. During a visit to Ankara by Egyptian President Hosni Mubarak in March 2007, the leaders of the two countries decided to establish a new strategic dialogue and partnership. The new strategic dialogue will focus in particular on energy cooperation and ways to strengthen regional security.

The improvement in Turkey's relations with Saudi Arabia and Egypt highlights the way in which Turkey has begun to reach out to leading Sunni Arab states in the Middle East and also provides another example of Turkey's new regional activism. The driving force behind this enhanced cooperation, however, has been strategic, not religious. It reflects the growing recognition on the part of the Turkish leadership that stability on the country's southern border requires Turkey's active engagement with its Middle Eastern neighbors and deeper participation in regional peace efforts.

Growing Ties to the Gulf Cooperation Council

Turkey has significantly expanded its relations with the members of the Gulf Cooperation Council (GCC), especially in the economic area. Turkey's trade with GCC members has soared in the last few years. In the first eight months of 2008, Turkey's exports to Kuwait rose 172 percent, those to Qatar rose 203 percent, and those to the United Arab Emirates increased 210 percent. For the first time, the United

Arab Emirates edged out Germany as the top export destination for Turkish goods.[11]

This trade activity is part of the Erdoğan government's conscious strategy to diversify Turkey's export markets and reduce the country's reliance on the EU. The EU is still Turkey's largest trading partner, accounting for half of all Turkish exports. However, the percentage of its exports to the EU has declined from 56 percent when the AKP took power in 2002 to about 50 percent in 2008.

At the same time, Turkey has increasingly become a magnet for Gulf-based investors. According to figures from the Turkish Treasury, the number of Gulf-based firms investing in Turkey has more than doubled since 2003.[12] Whereas in 2003 there was no Gulf-based capital invested in Turkey, in 2006, Gulf-based capital invested in Turkey reached $1.78 billion. Much of this investment has occurred in the agricultural sector and aims to increase strategic food reserves.

In September 2008, Turkey and the GCC countries signed an MOU making Turkey the first country outside the Gulf to be given the status of a strategic partner. The MOU represents a qualitative enhancement of Turkish-GCC relations and lays the foundation for a regular dialogue at the foreign-minister level. The MOU is expected to give new impetus to the dialogue on the creation of a free trade zone, a topic that has been under discussion since 2005.

For Turkey, the Gulf represents an important market for Turkish products. Turkey has also presented itself as a source of water, which would be transported from Turkey to the Arabian Peninsula through the so-called pipeline of peace. The GCC's interest in Turkey is both economic and political. With high oil prices resulting in windfalls in revenue in 2003–2007, the GCC countries began looking for a place to invest, and Turkey was seen as an attractive market for those investments. The GCC countries also see Turkey as an important regional power that can balance Iran.

---

[11] Pelin Turgut, "Exports: Trade with Middle East Soars as Relationships Thaw," *Financial Times* (London), November 28, 2008.

[12] Ebru Tuncay, "Turkey the Winner in Gulf's Investment Hunt," *Hürriyet Daily News and Economic Review* (Istanbul), September 1, 2008.

The Israeli Connection

Since 1996, close ties to Israel, especially in the defense and intelligence areas, have been one of the cornerstones of Turkish policy in the Middle East. However, Turkish policy toward Israel has begun to change under the AKP. The Erdoğan government has pursued a much more openly pro-Palestinian policy than its recent predecessors. Erdoğan has been strongly critical of Israeli policy in the West Bank and Gaza, calling Israeli policy an act of "state terror."[13]

The Israeli offensive in Gaza in December 2008–January 2009 provoked an even-harsher Turkish reaction. During a panel discussion at the World Economic Forum in Davos, Switzerland, in January 2009, Erdoğan got into a shouting match with Israeli President Simon Peres over the Israeli offensive and angrily stalked off the stage when he was not allowed to finish his criticism of the Israeli actions, causing a major international stir. Although both sides have since tried to play down the incident, Erdoğan's outburst damaged Turkey's reputation and raised questions in the minds of many Israeli officials about Turkey's reliability as a partner.

In addition, the Erdoğan government has sought to establish closer ties to the Palestinian leadership. A few weeks after the January 2006 elections in the Palestinian territories, Turkey hosted a high-ranking Hamas delegation led by Khaled Mashaal in Ankara. The visit was supposed to showcase Turkey's ability to play a larger diplomatic role in the Middle East. However, it was arranged without consulting Washington and Jerusalem, and it provoked strong irritation in both capitals because it directly undercut U.S. and Israeli efforts to isolate Hamas until it meets a series of specific conditions, including acceptance of Israel's right to exist.

The shift in Turkish policy toward Israel has largely been one of tone and style rather than substance. Although Erdoğan has been critical of Israeli policy, beneath the surface, Turkish-Israeli cooperation in the defense and intelligence areas has quietly continued. A $165-million agreement on airborne imagery intelligence was signed on the eve of

---

[13] "Israeli Operation Draws Ire in Turkey," *The Probe* (Istanbul), May 23, 2004.

the Gaza bombardment. The Israeli Air Force continues to conduct training missions at Turkey's training base in Konya. Turkey also participated with Israel and the United States in the annual joint exercise Reliant Mermaid in August 2009.[14]

In private, however, there is growing concern among Israeli officials about Turkey's increasing involvement in the Palestinian issue, and especially Turkey's support for Hamas. Israeli officials still want strong relations with Turkey, but the growing anti-Israel tone of Erdoğan's rhetoric is deeply worrisome to many Israeli officials and is beginning to have a corrosive impact on the overall relationship, eroding trust and confidence in Ankara's long-term objectives in the Middle East.[15] Because of its close ties to Hamas, Turkey is no longer regarded by Israeli leaders as an honest broker and a potential mediator in the Arab-Israeli dispute. The Netanyahu government has also spurned Turkey's offer to resume its role in facilitating talks between Israel and Syria.[16]

Although the Turkish-Israeli relationship has lost some of its early luster, it still retains importance for both sides. For Turkey, Israel is a valuable source of sophisticated military equipment and intelligence, while, for Israel, Turkey provides valuable training sites for the Israeli Air Force that would be difficult to replace. Thus, neither side is likely to allow relations to deteriorate too badly.

However, the likelihood that Turkish-Israeli relations will recover their early luster is slim, especially while the Netanyahu government is in power in Israel. Indeed, if anything, relations seem likely to get worse. The two governments have deep differences over a number of key

---

[14] Yaavov Katz, "Navy to Partake in Turkish Exercise," *Jerusalem Post*, August 11, 2009.

[15] One small sign of the changing tenor of relations has been the visible decline in the number of Israeli tourists visiting Turkey. The number of Israeli tourists visiting Antalya in the first six months of 2009 declined by 65 percent in comparison to the previous year. Although some of the decline may be due to the world economic crisis, Turkish press reports also cite Erdoğan's outburst at Davos as one of the primary causes of the sharp decline. See "Fewer Israeli Tourists After Davos Outburst," *Hürriyet Daily News and Economic Review* (Istanbul), June 14, 2009.

[16] Fulya Özerkan, "Israel Snubs Offer of Channel to Syria," *Hürriyet Daily News and Economic Review* (Istanbul), August 14, 2009. See also "Israel zeigt der Türkei die kalte Schulter," *Neue Zürcher Zeitung*, August 14, 2009.

international issues, especially Iran's possible acquisition of a nuclear-weapon capability, which Netanyahu sees as an existential threat to Israel's existence that must be prevented at all costs, including using military force if necessary. However, Turkey strongly opposes the use of force to resolve the Iranian nuclear issue. Thus, an Israeli military strike against Iran could lead to a serious crisis in Turkish-Israeli ties.

Democracy Promotion in the Middle East

Differences between Washington and Ankara have also emerged over the issue of democracy promotion in the Middle East. Although the Erdoğan government has been a strong advocate of greater transparency and democracy in the region, Turkish officials, especially the military, have been uncomfortable with U.S. attempts to portray Turkey as a model for Muslim countries in the Middle East. The military and the secular political establishment fear that such emphasis on Turkey's connection to the Middle East could weaken Turkey's Western identity and strengthen the role of Islam in Turkish society.[17]

Turkish officials insist that Turkey's path to democracy is not a one-size-fits-all model that can be implemented identically elsewhere in the Middle East. Although they contend that Turkey's path can serve as an "inspiration" or point of reference for other Muslim societies, they emphasize that the Muslim countries in the Middle East have to "find their own solutions to their own problems" and that these solutions cannot be imposed from outside.[18]

---

[17] In a toughly worded statement in April 2005 clearly aimed at the United States, Chief of the General Staff General Hilmi Özkök bluntly rejected the idea that Turkey could serve as a model for other Islamic countries, noting that "some circles try to define Turkey as a moderate Islamic country which could be an example for other Islamic countries. Turkey is not an Islamic country but a secular, democratic and social state that has adopted the rule of law" ("Ozkok Talks Tough," *Turkish Daily News* (Istanbul), April 21, 2005). Özkök's remarks reflected the Turkish military's strong discomfort with U.S. efforts to depict Turkey as a model for other Islamic countries. See also "Ozkok: Turkei kein Modell," *Frankfurter Allgemeine Zeitung*, April 22, 2005.

[18] See Abdullah Gül, "Turkey's Role in a Changing Middle East Environment," *Mediterranean Quarterly*, Vol. 15, No. 1, Winter 2004, pp. 2–7. See also Prime Minister Erdoğan's

In part, Turkey's differences with the United States over the idea of the country serving as a model for the Middle East reflect the Erdoğan government's desire to avoid steps that could complicate Turkey's relations with its Arab neighbors in the Middle East or lead to greater instability in the region. But they also reflect broader internal tensions within Turkish society between secularists—particularly the military—and Islamists. The military is highly sensitive to any developments that might weaken Turkey's adherence to secularism, and it is likely to continue to see any attempt by the United States to promote Turkey as a model for other Islamic countries as a threat to Turkey's secular identity.[19]

---

speech to the Oxford Centre for Islamic Studies in early April 2009. In this speech, Erdoğan explicitly rejected the idea of Turkey as a representative of "moderate Islam." See "Prime Minister Objects to 'Moderate Islam' Label," *Hürriyet Daily News and Economic Review* (Istanbul), April 4–5, 2009.

[19] In his speech to the Turkish parliament in April 2009, Obama was careful to address both sides of the religious divide, and he avoided singling out Turkey as a model for other Muslim countries in the Middle East—a decision that was strongly welcomed by Turkish secularists.

CHAPTER FIVE

Russia and Eurasia

Since the end of the Cold War, Central Asia has emerged as an important focal point of Turkish foreign policy. This concern with Central Asia represents a significant shift in Turkey's foreign policy. Under President Mustafa Kemal Atatürk, Turkey consciously eschewed efforts to cultivate contacts with the Turkic and Muslim populations beyond its borders. The closed nature of the Soviet system and Russian sensitivities about maintaining control over non-Russian nationalities also made communication and contact with the peoples of Central Asia difficult. As a result, this area was largely off-limits to Turkish diplomacy for much of the 20th century.

The collapse of the Soviet Union, however, opened new opportunities—and new challenges—for Turkish diplomacy. With the collapse of the Soviet Union, a whole new "Turkic world," previously closed to Turkish policy, opened up. Turkish politicians, especially Özal, saw Central Asia as a "new frontier" for expanding Turkish influence and enhancing Turkey's strategic importance.[1] At the same time, Turkish leaders saw the opening of Central Asia as a way to offset Turkey's difficulties with Europe.

However, the initial hopes that Central Asia would be a new El Dorado for Turkish diplomacy proved to be exaggerated. Having just emerged from decades of Soviet domination, the countries of Central Asia were not ready to replace one "big brother" with another. Turkey

---

[1] For a comprehensive discussion, see F. Stephen Larrabee and Ian O. Lesser, *Turkish Foreign Policy in an Age of Uncertainty*, Santa Monica, Calif.: RAND Corporation, MR-1612-CMEPP, 2003, pp. 99–126.

also initially overestimated the attractiveness of the Turkish model for Central Asia: Although many Central Asian leaders admired Turkey's economic progress, few wished to emulate its pluralistic democratic system, which would have weakened their own autocratic powers.

Russian influence in Central Asia also proved stronger and more enduring than Turkish officials had anticipated. Russian President Boris Yeltsin paid scant attention to Central Asia and allowed Russia's ties to the region to atrophy. However, President Vladimir Putin and his successor, President Dmitry Medvedev, have given high priority to strengthening ties to Central Asia, particularly economic ties. Russia's political and economic influence in Central Asia are thus much stronger today than during the Yeltsin era.

As a result, Turkey found making political and economic inroads in Central Asia harder than it initially expected. Although Central Asia remains an important area of Turkish interest, the initial euphoria evident under Özal has been tempered by a greater sense of realism about the prospects for expanding Turkish influence in the region.

The Russian Factor

Turkey's relations with Russia have undergone an important shift since the end of the Cold War. Historically, Russia and Turkey have been bitter enemies. Over the last several centuries, they have fought 13 wars against each other, most of which Turkey lost. This historical animosity was reinforced by Stalin's aggressive policy toward Turkey early in the Cold War, which was the driving force behind Turkey's decision to join NATO in 1952.

In the last decade, however, Turkey's relations with Russia have improved markedly, especially in the economic realm. Russia is Turkey's largest trading partner and its largest supplier of natural gas. Russia is also an important market for the Turkish construction industry. Projects in Russia account for about one-fourth of all projects carried out by Turkish contractors around the world.

Energy has been an important driver of the recent intensification of ties between Ankara and Moscow. Russia supplies 65 percent of Turkey's natural-gas imports and 40 percent of its crude-oil imports. Turkish officials have suggested that, if current trends continue, natural-gas imports from Russia could increase to 80 percent in the coming decade. Russian investment in Turkey, especially in the energy, tourism, and telecommunication sectors, has also grown visibly in recent years.

Political ties between the two countries have warmed as well.[2] In December 2004, Putin became the first Russian head of State to visit Turkey in 32 years. The visit was crowned by a joint declaration on the "Deepening of Friendship and Multi-Dimensional Partnership," which makes reference to a wide range of common interests and to the mutual trust and confidence that have developed between the two countries in recent years. Since then, high-level political contacts between Ankara and Moscow have visibly increased.

The closer ties between Ankara and Moscow that have emerged in the last decade, especially in the economic area, have made Turkey more sensitive to Russian concerns in the Caucasus/Central Asia. Indeed, on a number of issues related to Central Asian and Caspian security, Ankara's position is closer to Moscow's than to Washington's. For example, Ankara showed little enthusiasm for the Bush administration's efforts to promote democracy in Central Asia. Like Moscow, Ankara feared that U.S. attempts to press the regimes in the region to democratize could destabilize the regimes and lead to increased regional turbulence and political unrest.

As Turkey's relations with the United States and Europe have become more strained, some Turkish strategists have begun to look to Russia as a possible strategic alternative.[3] Although voices favoring an alliance with Russia represent a minority view, support for this position has grown in recent years. As Burak Bekdil has noted, "What could have been brushed away as an 'eccentric, insane idea' surprisingly finds

[2] For a detailed discussion, see Suat Kınıklıoğlu, "The Anatomy of Turkish-Russian Relations," *Insight Turkey*, Vol. 8, No. 2, April–June 2006.

[3] See General Tuncer Kılınç, speech at the War Academy, Istanbul, March 7, 2002. When he gave the speech, Kılınç was secretary of the Turkish National Security Council.

many cautious and non-cautious supporters in several gray office build-ings in Ankara."[4]

However, a serious strategic realignment away from the West toward Russia is unlikely for several reasons. First, despite the recent improvement in Turkish-Russian relations, mistrust of Russia is deeply embedded in the Turkish historical consciousness. Second, Turkish and Russian goals and ambitions conflict in a number of areas, and particularly the Caucasus (a region in which Turkey has deep and long-standing strategic interests). These conflicting interests and goals make any serious realignment unlikely.

Third, Russia and Turkey are energy competitors in the Caspian and Central Asia. Russia wants to control the distribution and export lines of energy resources in those regions and has opposed such schemes as the Transcaspian and Nabucco pipelines, projects that would pro-vide alternative means for exporting the region's energy resources to Europe. Turkey, however, strongly favors both initiatives and hopes to become a hub for the transport of natural gas to Europe.

Fourth, and perhaps most important, a realignment toward Russia would represent a repudiation of the policy of Westernization that has been the cornerstone of Turkish policy since the founding of the Turk-ish Republic by Atatürk in 1923. Such a radical departure from the fundamental principles of Kemalism would be anathema to the major-ity of Turks—and, above all, to the Turkish military, which sees itself as the guardian of Atatürk's legacy.

In the aftermath of the Russian invasion of Georgia, Turkish-Russian relations will be strongly affected by the evolution of Russia's broader ties to the West, especially the United States. Ankara has a strong stake in a benign climate between Washington and Moscow. As Lesser has noted, Turkey's ability to conduct a policy of breadth rather than depth—to engage diverse partners with conflicting inter-ests simultaneously—would be severely constrained by more-overt

---

[4]   Burak Bekdil, "An Incursion Which Is Not—and Russophiles in Ankara," *Turkish Daily News* (Istanbul), June 8, 2007.

competition between Russia and the West.[5] Since the end of the Cold War, Turkey has had the luxury of not having to choose between its Western and Eurasian interests. However, a sharpening of U.S.-Russian competition would make it more difficult for Turkey to balance these competing interests, particularly in the Caucasus, and increase the pressure on Ankara to choose.

The global economic crisis could also have a negative impact on Turkey's economic relations with Russia. As a result of the crisis, credit in Russia has dried up, and investors have refrained from making investments. Turkish construction firms operating in Russia have been particularly hard-hit by the crisis. A large number of Turkish projects have come to a standstill or been forced to slow their pace, resulting in significant financial losses to Turkish firms.[6]

Turkish-Armenian Rapprochement

The five-day war between Russia and Georgia in August 2008 unleashed a new set of regional dynamics in the Caucasus. On the one hand, it shattered the old political balance in the region and strengthened Russia's role as an *Ordnungsmacht* [regional hegemon] in the Caucasus. On the other hand, it created new challenges for Ankara and sparked a new activism in Turkish policy toward the Caucasus designed to strengthen regional stability and mitigate the destabilizing political dynamics unleashed by the Russian invasion.

The most important manifestation of this new activism has been Ankara's attempt to improve relations with Yerevan. Relations with Armenia have been strained by two issues in particular: (1) Armenia's campaign to brand Turkey guilty of genocide for the mass deaths of Armenians in 1915 and (2) Armenia's invasion and occupation of Nagorno-Karabakh in Azerbaijan. In the aftermath of the Armenian

---

[5] Ian O. Lesser, "After Georgia: Turkey's Looming Foreign Policy Dilemmas," *On Turkey*, German Marshall Fund of the United States, August 26, 2008a, p. 2.

[6] Tuğba Tekerek, "Crisis Hits Turkish Projects in Russia," *Turkish Daily News* (Istanbul), October 18–19, 2008.

invasion, Ankara closed its border with Armenia and suspended efforts to establish diplomatic relations with Yerevan. Relations remained essentially frozen thereafter.

However, since the Russian invasion of Georgia in August 2008, Turkey has intensified its effort to improve relations with Armenia. This effort was given important new impetus by President Gül's historic visit to Yerevan in September 2008 to attend a football match between Turkey and Armenia. Gül's visit was the first visit ever to Armenia by a Turkish head of state, and it set off an intensive round of diplomacy aimed at normalizing bilateral relations.

On April 22, 2009, after more than a year of behind-the-scenes diplomatic talks, Turkey and Armenia released a joint statement saying that the two sides had agreed on a framework for a roadmap to normalize relations. Although the content of the roadmap was not publicly announced, it is believed to involve (1) the establishment of diplomatic representation in each country, (2) a gradual reopening of the Turkish-Armenian border, (3) Armenian recognition of Turkey's international borders, and (4) the establishment of a historical commission to investigate the disputed events of 1915.[7]

A normalization of Turkish-Armenian relations would have several important benefits: First, it would enable Armenia to reduce its economic and political dependence on Moscow. Second, it would give new impetus to Turkey's EU membership bid. Third, it would enable Armenia to be integrated into regional economic and energy schemes from which it is currently excluded. Finally, it would defuse pressure to pass the Armenian Genocide Resolution currently before the House of Representatives (a topic discussed in more detail in the next section).

However, normalization of relations with Armenia is far from a done deal. The growing rapprochement between Turkey and Armenia

---

[7] The timing of the publication of the joint statement—two days before the celebration of Armenian Remembrance Day, a day on which the U.S. president traditionally issues a statement commemorating the mass deaths of the Armenians killed in 1915—suggests that the joint statement was primarily designed to forestall the use of the word "genocide" in Obama's statement and defuse the genocide issue in advance of Obama's trip to Turkey on April 6–8, 2009.

has caused serious strains in Turkey's relations with Azerbaijan. Baku fears that it will lose important leverage in the negotiations with Armenia over Nagorno-Karabakh if Ankara reestablishes diplomatic ties to Yerevan, and it has linked its support for Turkish-Armenian rapprochement to prior progress toward a settlement of the Nagorno-Karabakh issue.[8]

In an attempt to allay Azerbaijani concerns, Ankara has assured Baku that the Turkish-Armenian border will not be opened until Yerevan withdraws its troops from Nagorno-Karabakh.[9] Ankara sees the opening of the border and progress on Nagorno-Karabakh as parallel and mutually reinforcing processes. In effect, the pace of the implementation of the Turkish-Armenian roadmap has become linked to progress on resolving the Nagorno-Karabakh conflict. This is likely to complicate the process of normalization of Turkish-Armenian relations.

Russia could also pose an obstacle to full normalization of Turkish-Armenian relations. Normalization of Turkish-Armenian relations would reduce Yerevan's need for Moscow's support and open up prospects for Armenia to expand its ties to the West. Such a development is not in Russia's interest because it would reduce Moscow's leverage over Yerevan and its influence in the Caucasus more broadly. Thus, at some point, Moscow could decide that the rapprochement entails too many risks to its interests in the Caucasus and put pressure on Yerevan to retrench, causing the process of Turkish-Armenian reconciliation to cool or falter.

In addition, the reconciliation process faces internal opposition in both Turkey and Armenia. Turkish opposition parties and pressure groups have raised objections to the opening of the Turkish-Armenian border without some progress toward a resolution of the Nagorno-Karabakh issue. They have also accused the Erdoğan government of

---

[8] Emrullah Uslu, "Ankara-Yerevan Rapprochement Strains Turkey's Relations with Azerbaijan," *Eurasia Daily Monitor*, Vol. 6, No. 68, April 9, 2009b. See also Barçın Yinanc, "Outreach to Armenia Prompts Azeri Threat," *Hürriyet Daily News and Economic Review* (Istanbul), April 2, 2009.

[9] Emrullah Uslu, "Erdogan Reassures Azerbaijan on Turkey's Border Policy with Armenia," *Eurasia Daily Monitor*, Vol. 6, No. 93, May 14, 2009d.

neglecting the interests of Azerbaijan. The April 22 agreement has come under strong criticism from nationalist forces in Armenia as well.[10] Public-opinion surveys indicate that more than half of the population opposes the agreement.

The rapprochement was given new impetus with the joint announcement on August 31, 2009, that Turkey and Armenia had initialed two protocols.[11] In the first protocol on the establishment of diplomatic relations, the two sides promised to establish diplomatic relations on the first day of the first month after the ratification of the protocol and to open the border within two months of ratification of the protocol. In the second protocol on the development of bilateral relations, scheduled to go into effect simultaneously with the diplomatic opening, the two sides promised to promote cooperation in a variety of areas, from tourism to energy infrastructure. The protocols also commit the two sides to establishing a dialogue on the "historical dimension"—a code word for the emotionally charged dispute over the death of up to 1.5 million Armenians during the waning days of the Ottoman empire at the end of World War I.

The announcement is an important step in the process of reconciliation between Turkey and Armenia. This process is likely to take time and will have to be carefully managed, especially regarding its impact on Turkey's relations with Azerbaijan. However, if the steps in the joint statement are fully implemented, they could have important consequences not only for bilateral ties between Turkey and Armenia but also for the broader political dynamics in the Caucasus as well as Turkey's relations with the EU.

---

[10] For details, see "Die Türkei-Frage spaltet Armenien," *Neue Zürcher Zeitung*, May 13, 2009.

[11] "Armenians and Turks Have Far to Go on Genocide," *International Herald Tribune*, September 1, 2009.

The Armenian Genocide Resolution

The Turkish-Armenian rapprochement process is further complicated by the Armenian genocide issue in the U.S. Congress. The Armenian diaspora in the United States regularly seeks to introduce a resolution condemning Turkey for the death of hundreds of thousands of Armenians in 1915. These resolutions have been sharply condemned by the Turks and have been a source of serious discord in U.S.-Turkish relations. In the fall of 2007, the Bush administration narrowly averted a serious crisis with Ankara only by a last-minute, all-out lobbying campaign that prevented the Armenian Genocide Resolution (H.R. 106) from coming to a vote on the floor of the U.S. House of Representatives.

The resolution was introduced again in 2009. During the 2008 U.S. presidential campaign, Obama supported the resolution (as did Hillary Clinton). However, as president, Obama has given priority to strengthening ties to Turkey. During his visit to Turkey in April 2009, he encouraged Ankara to engage in a serious effort to address the historical issues surrounding the events of 1915, but he carefully avoided specific reference to genocide in his statement on Armenian Remembrance Day on April 24, 2009. This suggests that he is unlikely to support passage of the resolution in the near term.

Passage of a genocide resolution would deal a serious blow to the Obama administration's efforts to put U.S.-Turkish relations on a firmer footing, and it could prompt the Turks to take retaliatory action, including, potentially, imposing constraints on U.S. use of Turkish facilities. It could also seriously set back the process of Turkish-Armenian reconciliation currently under way and undermine the more open attitude toward addressing the Armenian issue that has been emerging in Turkey in the last few years.[12]

---

[12] At the end of 2008, a group of prominent Turkish intellectuals, academics, and journalists began circulating on the Internet an open letter expressing their sympathy for the Armenians killed in 1915 and inviting Turkish citizens to apologize for the mass deaths. Turkey has also opened its Ottoman archives pertaining to the period under question to scholars (foreign as well as Turkish) to enable them to better understand and evaluate the events of 1915. Beginning in 2009, Armenian language and literature will be taught at Turkish universities. See Şaban Kardaş, "Turkey Confronts a Disputed Period in Its History," *Eurasia Daily Monitor*, Vol. 5, No. 240, December 17, 2008.

The Broader Regional Dimension

Turkey's drive to improve relations with Armenia has been part of a broader effort by Ankara to enhance peace and stability in the Caucasus on a regional level. The centerpiece of this effort has been the Erdoğan government's initiative for a Caucasus Stability and Cooperation Platform. Launched in the immediate aftermath of the Russian invasion of Georgia, the platform is designed to enhance regional cooperation between Russia, Turkey, Georgia, Azerbaijan, and Armenia.

However, the initiative appears to have been slapped together rather quickly with little effort to coordinate it with key Western allies. Moreover, it has a number of weaknesses that are likely to limit its chances of success. First, having just suffered a Russian military invasion, Georgia has little interest in joining a regional scheme that could enhance Russia's economic and political involvement in the Caucasus.

The unresolved territorial conflict between Azerbaijan and Armenia over Nagorno-Karabakh poses a second important obstacle to the realization of the plan. Until there is significant progress toward resolving this issue, Azerbaijan is unlikely to show much interest in cooperation with Armenia.

Russia's recognition of the independence of the Georgian breakaway regions of Abkhazia and South Ossetia poses a third important obstacle that is likely to limit the success of the initiative. The Russian action sets a precedent for separatism that few countries in the region are willing to legitimize. This is particularly true for Turkey because recognition of the independence of Abkhazia and South Ossetia could encourage and legitimize Kurdish separatism in Turkey.

Fourth, the initiative does not include the United States, the EU, or Iran, all of which are important actors in the Caucasus. These actors do not appear to have been consulted before the initiative was launched, and their support for the initiative has been lukewarm at best. Hence, the initiative does not seem likely to meet with much immediate success. However, Turkish authorities regard it as an additional vehicle for engaging Armenia, and they hope that it may help promote greater regional cooperation over the long run.

The Energy Dimension

Energy is an important factor driving Turkish policy in the Caucasus and the Caspian region. The Russian invasion of Georgia and the Russian-Ukrainian gas conflict in early 2009 have underscored the need for Europe to shore up its energy security by diversifying its suppliers. and have contributed to increased interest within the EU in the Nabucco project, which would transport Caspian gas to Europe via a pipeline that would run from Turkey through Romania, Hungary, and Austria (see Figure 5.1).

However, the Nabucco project faces a number of obstacles that have raised questions about its viability. The most serious problem is finding sufficient gas to make the pipeline commercially viable. To date, only Azerbaijan has committed to supplying gas for the pipeline. But Baku can supply only a fraction of the pipeline's capacity. To be commercially viable, Nabucco needs to find other suppliers that will contribute toward its annual transport capacity of 31 bcm.

Figure 5.1
The Nabucco Pipeline

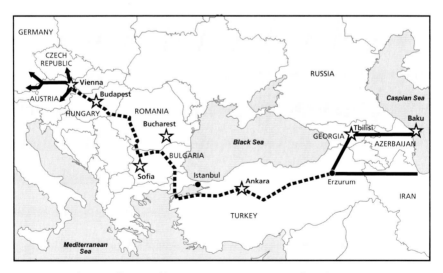

SOURCE: Sémhur, Atelier Graphique, GNU Free Documentation License.
RAND *MG899-5.1*

Some EU officials suggest that Iran could make up some of the shortfall. However, this option is a nonstarter as long as the United States and the EU remain locked in a standoff over Iran's nuclear program. Unless there is a change in Iran's nuclear policy, U.S. officials have ruled out Iran as a supplier for Nabucco.

Turkmenistan is another potential supplier. At the moment, Russia has a near-monopoly on gas exports from Turkmenistan. However, Turkmenistan has been locked in a pricing dispute with Gazprom and is looking to diversify its exports. The recent discovery of new reserves in Turkmenistan opens the prospect that in the second half of this decade, Turkmenistan could ship some of its gas via the Nabucco pipeline, which would help reduce the current shortfall. Iraq and Qatar are also possible suppliers.

Russia has tried to prevent the realization of the Nabucco project by offering to buy all of Azerbaijan's available export volumes of gas from 2009 onward. So far, Baku has refused Moscow's offer because it would undermine Azerbaijan's energy partnership with the West and severely curtail its national independence. However, Baku appears to be keeping its options open. At the end of March 2009, the State Oil Company of Azerbaijan signed an MOU with Gazprom for the development of cooperation on natural gas.[13] If the MOU leads to a serious expansion of cooperation with Moscow, Baku could begin shipping the bulk of its gas via Russia by 2010. This would deal a strong blow to Nabucco's viability and to Turkey's hopes of becoming an important transit route for the export of Caspian gas to Europe.

Moscow has also sought to undercut Nabucco by proposing the construction of the South Stream pipeline, which would run along a route to Europe similar to Nabucco's and would target the same group of countries. The South Stream pipeline would flood the gas market in southeastern Europe, locking up the customers upon whom the bankers behind Nabucco are counting to finance the EU-backed project. In

---

[13] Stephen Blank, "Azerbaijan: Russia Is Increasingly Nervous About Its Grip on Caspian Energy," *Eurasia Insight*, Eurasianet.org, March 30, 2009. See also Roman Kupchinsky, "Azerbaijan and Russia Ink Tentative Gas Agreement," *Eurasia Daily Monitor*, Vol. 6, No. 62, April 1, 2009.

addition, Russia has tried to obtain control of oil and gas pipelines and refineries on EU territory.[14]

Nabucco has also been plagued by internal squabbles within the EU over financing the project. At a high-level meeting in Budapest on January 26–27, 2009, the European Commission and EU-funded lending institutions announced plans to support Nabucco. However, at an informal summit in Brussels at the beginning of March 2009, German Chancellor Angela Merkel blocked EU funding for Nabucco on the grounds that there were enough private lenders for the project.[15] Some funds for Nabucco were later restored, but it is unclear whether, as the full impact of the current global economic crisis begins to be felt, the EU will find sufficient funds to finance the project.

Turkey's actions have also contributed to delays in the project. Turkey has sought to use the transit issue as a means of leverage in its broader relationship with the EU. Ankara has demanded the right to buy 15 percent of the transit gas that would pass through Turkey en route to Europe. This "lift-off" portion then could be resold or used for domestic consumption. Turkey has also demanded higher taxes and transit fees than other consortium members.

However, Nabucco's prospects have been given a boost by several developments. On July 13, 2009, Bulgaria, Romania, Hungary, and Austria signed an intergovernmental transit agreement with Turkey.[16] The agreement is expected to give Nabucco new impetus and enhance its credibility with suppliers. In addition, Iraq has offered to supply

---

[14] At the end of March 2009, the Kremlin-controlled Surgut Neftegaz became the largest shareholder in the MOL Hungarian Oil and Gas Company. MOL owns the most-efficient refineries in Central Europe and is the dominant stakeholder in Croatia's gas and oil company, INA. It is also a partner in the Nabucco project. Thus, control of MOL would give Russia an important means of influencing the European energy market, including the fate of Nabucco. See Vladimir Socor, "The Strategic Implications of Russian Move Against Hungary's MOL," *Eurasia Daily Monitor*, Vol. 6, No. 77, April 22, 2009b.

[15] Vladimir Socor, "Chancellor Merkel Says Nein to Nabucco," *Eurasia Daily Monitor*, Vol. 6, No. 45, March 9, 2009a. See also "Nabucco Project Not in EU Pipeline," *Hürriyet Daily News and Economic Review* (Istanbul), March 18, 2009.

[16] Sabrina Tavernise and Sebnem Arsu, "Gas Pipeline Through Turkey Gains Backing in Europe," *New York Times*, July 14, 2009.

15 bcm of gas—nearly half of the 31 bcm of gas needed for Nabucco to operate at full capacity.[17] Turkmenistan has also offered to ship some of its gas via Nabucco in the second stage. In addition, falling commodity and steel prices have reduced the estimated cost of building the pipeline, enhancing the prospects that the project will receive the necessary financing.

Turkey stands to be one of the major beneficiaries if Nabucco is eventually built. The pipeline will enhance Turkey's role as an important regional actor and make Turkey a key cog in Europe's effort to achieve energy independence. It will also enable Turkey to expand its influence with its immediate neighbors, especially Iran and Iraq. There will be important economic benefits as well. As a pivotal transit country—more than half of the pipeline will be on Turkish soil—Turkey will receive 60 percent of the tax revenues. The pipeline is also expected to attract infrastructure investment and create new jobs.

However, Nabucco is not a done deal. Offers from Iraq and Turkmenistan to ship gas via Nabucco would, if implemented, go a long way toward solving the supply problem. But, many energy experts question whether Iraq can be considered a reliable supplier, given Iraq's disputes with the KRG over sharing energy resources and revenue. If the tensions between the KRG and the central government in Baghdad escalate, the Maliki government could find it difficult to make good on its offer to supply the 15 bcm of gas it has offered to transport via Nabucco. Turkmenistan is also far from a reliable supplier and could come under strong Russian pressure not to supply gas to Nabucco.

Still, although a number of uncertainties and obstacles remain, the prospects that Nabucco will eventually be built have significantly improved. The project has gained new momentum with the signing of the July 13, 2009, intergovernmental agreement, and it has strong political support, both in Brussels and in Washington. And Russia's decision to cut off gas to Ukraine, which left much of Southern and Eastern Europe to face a bitter winter with no gas for weeks, has strengthened the determination of many European nations to reduce

---

[17] Delphine Strauss and Ed Cooks, "Iraq Offers Half Gas Needed for Nabucco," *Financial Times* (London), July 13, 2009.

their dependence on Russian energy, particularly natural gas. This adds an important new political-psychological dimension that increases the chances that Nabucco will eventually be built.

At the same time, Turkey has kept open the door to cooperation with Russia. The set of energy agreements signed by Erdoğan and Putin during Putin's visit to Ankara on August 6, 2009, gave a boost to the Russian-sponsored South Stream pipeline, which Moscow has promoted as an alternative to Nabucco, and they reinforce the growing economic and political ties between Russia and Turkey that have developed in the last decade. The South Stream pipeline would allow Russia to bypass Ukraine, through which 80 percent of Russian energy exports to Europe currently traverse, thus reducing Ukraine's ability to cut off Russian energy supplies to Europe.

But South Stream faces a number of major logistical and financial obstacles that make its construction and commercial viability highly uncertain. The natural gas has to be transported from the Russian Black Sea port of Novorossiysk via a 560-mile pipeline underneath the Black Sea, and it must then be transported long distances over land to reach Italy and Austria. Constructing such a vast pipeline is no mean feat. Moreover, it is unclear who will foot the bill for the construction of the pipeline, which is estimated to cost $10 billion–$30 billion. This is a huge sum, and the expense comes at a time when Russia's energy industry has been badly hurt by the global economic crisis. Thus, South Stream's viability over the long turn remains an open question.

Nevertheless, the signing of the August 6, 2009, agreements with Moscow underscores both the increasingly important strategic role that Turkey has begun to play as a transit route in European and Eurasian energy schemes and the importance of Turkey's growing economic ties to Russia. These ties bear close monitoring. Although they increase Turkey's strategic significance as a regional actor, they also give Ankara a strong stake in maintaining good political ties to Moscow. It is a delicate balancing act, and if there is a downturn in the West's relations with Russia, it could become increasingly difficult to maintain.

CHAPTER SIX

The European Dimension

The recent strains in U.S.-Turkish relations have been compounded by growing problems in Turkey's relations with Europe, particularly the EU. For Turkey, EU membership has always been about more than economics: It represents a historical and "civilizational" choice—the culmination, in Turkish eyes, of the process of Westernization that began in the late 19th century under the Ottomans and was given irreversible impetus with the founding of the Turkish Republic by Atatürk in 1923. Hence, Turkey rejects the privileged-partnership idea advocated by some EU members, such as France, because that alternative implies less-than-full acceptance of Turkey's Western identity.

However, Turkish membership poses major challenges to the EU's absorptive capacity and political cohesion. With a population of close to 70 million, Turkey is the second-largest country in Europe. If its population continues to grow at the current rate, it will have the largest population in Europe by the middle of the 21st century. Integrating a country of this size—especially one characterized by great regional disparities and a per-capita income well below the EU average—would require major adjustments in EU institutions and policies.

Cultural factors also affect the membership question. There has always been—and continues to be—a sense among many Europeans that Turkey is not really European. As Iver Neumann has noted, for centuries, the Turk was the significant "other" against which Europe defined its identity.[1] This perception of Turks as "other" is deeply

---

[1] See Iver B. Neumann, *Uses of the Other: The "East" in European Identity Formation*, Minneapolis: University of Minnesota Press, 1999.

embedded in Europeans' collective consciousness and continues to color European views of Turkey today. Because of its Muslim culture and religion, Turkey is regarded by many EU members as not quite European.[2]

This ambiguity about Turkey's place in Europe—its "Europeanness"—has become more acute since the end of the Cold War. During the Cold War, military-strategic considerations tended to dominate Turkey's relationship to Europe. Other considerations were subordinated to the overriding strategic need to bind Turkey close to the West. Turkey provided a critical barrier to the expansion of Soviet military power into the Mediterranean. In addition, it tied down 24 Soviet divisions that would otherwise have been deployed on the Central Front.

However, with the disappearance of the Soviet threat and the transformation of the European Economic Community—as the EU was called in the 1960s—into the EU, cultural and social factors have become more-important considerations affecting membership, while the significance of military-strategic factors has declined. At the same time, with the addition of 12 new members since May 2004, questions about Europe's borders and identity—e.g., Where does Europe end? How far should the EU expand?—have begun to play a more prominent role in the debate about further enlargement and Turkish membership.

The Changing Turkish Domestic Context

The AKP has made Turkey's EU membership one of the main pillars of its foreign policy. The AKP's strong support for EU membership represents an important shift in the political orientation and agenda of the Islamic movement in Turkey, which traditionally opposed membership in the EU and pursued an anti-Western agenda. Under the leadership of Erdoğan and Gül, the AKP has jettisoned the anti-Western ideologi-

---

[2] In a poll conducted by the German Marshall Fund in 2008, over half the European respondents (57 percent) agreed that Turkey has such different values that it is not part of the West. The highest levels of agreement came from Germany (76 percent), France (68 percent), and Italy (61 percent). See Transatlantic Trends, 2008, p. 21.

cal rhetoric and tenets of its Islamic predecessors, the National Salvation Party and the Welfare Party, and has embraced a political agenda that emphasizes democracy, respect for human rights, rule of law, and membership in the EU and NATO.[3] Whereas in the past, Islamists in Turkey regarded Western calls for greater democratic reforms as an attempt to impose alien values on Turkey, the AKP leadership sees membership in the EU, with that organization's emphasis on democracy and human rights, as providing the best means of reducing the political influence of the Turkish military and establishing a more open political order that will ensure the survival of the party.

The AKP's strong support of Turkey's membership in the EU represents an important transformation of the Turkish political landscape. For decades, the Turkish military and the CHP were the champions of Westernization and close ties to Europe. In recent years, however, this role has been usurped by the AKP. The AKP has become the chief advocate of EU membership, while the military and the CHP have expressed increasing reservations about the pace of EU integration and some of its requirements, particularly enhanced rights for the Kurds and greater civilian control of the military.

European Attitudes Toward Turkish Membership

Whether Turkey will ever become a member of the EU is, at this stage, unclear. The EU Council agreed to open accession negotiations with Turkey at its summit in Brussels in December 2004. However, the council combined its assent with a number of caveats and escape clauses, noting that the initiation of negotiations did not guarantee their successful completion or preclude other forms of association short of membership.

Since then, opposition to Turkish membership has visibly increased, especially in France, Germany, and Austria. According to a *Financial Times*/Harris poll in June 2007, 71 percent of French citizens and

---

[3] For a detailed discussion of the AKP's ideological transformation, see Rabasa and Larrabee, 2008, especially pp. 31–50.

66 percent of German citizens oppose Turkish membership in the EU (see Figure 6.1).[4] Public opposition to Turkish membership remains strong, moreover, even if Turkey carries out reforms desired by EU members (see Figure 6.2).

This growing popular opposition to Turkey's EU membership has significantly complicated Turkey's membership aspirations and led to some rethinking within the EU about future relations with Turkey. Merkel and French President Nicolas Sarkozy have advocated a privileged partnership with Turkey. However, Turkey has rejected this option because it falls short of full membership, which remains the official Turkish goal.

In addition, the AKP's Islamic roots have cast the religious issue in starker relief. Is the EU willing to accept a predominantly Muslim country into its midst? Although few European leaders are willing to

Figure 6.1
European Public Opinion: Should Turkey Be Invited to Join the EU?

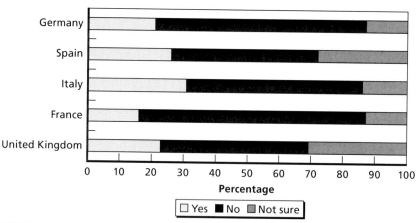

SOURCE: Harris Interactive, "Financial Times/Harris Poll: EU Citizens Want Referendum on Treaty," Web page, June 18, 2007. The Harris Interactive survey was carried out between May 31 and June 12, 2007. The question was asked of 6,169 total respondents in six countries: the United Kingdom (1,025), Germany (1,014), France (1,012), Italy (1,090), Spain (1,010), and the United States (1,018).
RAND MG899-6.1

---

[4] See "Public Opposition to Turkey's Entry Growing Stronger in the EU," *Today's Zaman* (Istanbul), June 19, 2007.

Figure 6.2
European Public Opinion: If Turkey Were to Implement Reforms Desired by Some EU Member States, Should It Be Invited to Join the EU?

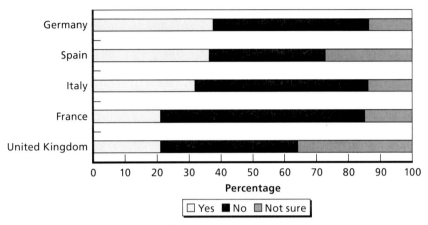

SOURCE: Harris Interactive, 2007. The Harris Interactive survey was carried out between May 31 and June 12, 2007. The question was asked of 4,526 respondents in six countries: the United Kingdom (769), Germany (839), France (751), Italy (726), Spain (786), and the United States (655).

RAND *MG899-6.2*

openly discuss this issue, it is an important issue for many EU citizens and affects the tenor of the debate about Turkish EU membership. As former Dutch Foreign Minister Hans Van Mierlo noted some years ago, "There is a problem of a large Muslim state. Do we want that in Europe? It is an unspoken question."[5]

This question has taken on greater resonance since 9/11, particularly in Germany, which has close to 3 million Turks living on its soil. Many of these Turks came to Germany in the 1960s as *Gastarbeiter* [guest workers] at a time when Germany faced a labor shortage, particularly in areas requiring unskilled labor. It was expected that these migrant workers would work in Germany for a few years and then return home. However, instead of returning, many stayed in Germany, creating in many German cities large ghettos of Turks who are permanent residents but are not well integrated into German society.

---

[5] Quoted in Stephen Kinzer, "Turkey Finds European Door Slow to Open," *New York Times*, February 23, 1997.

This has led to a growing debate in Germany about integration and multiculturalism.[6] Initially, the main obstacle to integration was the unwillingness of German authorities to acknowledge that the Turkish "temporary" workers were becoming a permanent fixture. Since 2000, the German authorities have shown a greater readiness to extend German citizenship to long-term Turkish residents. However, the stringent integration requirements remain an important obstacle to the acquisition of German citizenship by many Turks living in Germany, and they act as a brake on the integration process.[7]

Waning Turkish Support for EU Membership

The increasing popular opposition in Europe to Turkish membership in the EU has been accompanied by growing disenchantment in Turkey with the EU. Public support in Turkey for the country's EU membership, although still solid, has declined visibly over the last several years. Whereas in 2004, 73 percent of the Turkish population supported Turkish membership, that figure dropped to 54 percent in 2006 and to 40 percent in 2007.[8] This sharp decline illustrates how strongly the Turkish public's mood toward the EU has soured lately. This is true even among traditionally Western-oriented Turks.

---

[6]   See Stefan Luft, "Assimilation, Integration, Identität," *Frankfurter Allgemeine Zeitung*, in German, February 15, 2008. See also an interview with the Minister of Integration in Nordrhein-Westfalen Armin Laschet, "Kein Assimilationsdruck," *Frankfurter Allgemeine Zeitung*, February 13, 2008; Erdoğan's speech to the Turkish community in Cologne in February 2007 in "Erdogan's Kölner Rede," *Frankfurter Allgemeine Zeitung*, February 15, 2008. In his speech, Erdoğan condemned the idea of assimilation as a "crime against humanity" and requested that Turkish schools and universities be opened for Turks living in Germany—a request that was publicly rejected by Merkel. See "Merkel: Ich bin auch Kanzlerin der Turken in Deutschland," *Frankfurter Allgemeine Zeitung*, February 12, 2008. For a French view of the debate, see "Angela Merkel et Recep Tayyip Erdogan s'affrontent sur l'intégration des Turcs d'Allemagne," *Le Monde* (Paris), February 14, 2008.

[7]   See International Crisis Group, "Islam and Identity in Germany," Europe Report No. 181, Washington, D.C.: International Crisis Group, March 14, 2007a.

[8]   Transatlantic Trends, 2007, p. 22.

Several interrelated factors have contributed to this decline in public and elite support for Turkey's EU membership. The intense debate in Europe after the EU's Brussels summit in December 2004 regarding Turkey's European credentials provoked a nationalist backlash and strengthened the hand of antireform elements in Turkey. The fact that such key European leaders as Sarkozy and Merkel began questioning Turkey's credentials for membership after the accession negotiations had already been opened was seen by many Turks as proof of the EU's bias against Turkey and significantly contributed to the growing anti-EU mood among the Turkish public.

Domestic factors also played a role. The decision of the European Court of Human Rights to uphold the headscarf ban at Turkish universities, for instance, came as a rude shock to many AKP party members and dimmed support for EU membership within the AKP. Many AKP members had supported EU membership largely because they expected it would strengthen religious freedom. They were disillusioned by the court's decision, which seemed to call into question one of Turkey's basic rationales for joining the EU.

The EU's handling of the Cyprus issue also contributed to souring Turkish enthusiasm for EU membership. The Turks saw evidence of the EU's bias against and unfair treatment of Turkey in two Cyprus-related developments. First, the EU failed to keep its promise to lift its trade embargo against the Turkish Republic of Northern Cyprus (TRNC) despite the Turkish Cypriots' strong support for the UN-sponsored Annan plan—which the Greek Cypriots rejected—in the May 2004 referendum. Second, the EU decided in December 2006 to suspend eight chapters of the accession negotiations with Turkey because Turkey refused to open its ports and airports to Cypriot vessels.

Taken together, these factors have contributed to a slowdown in the process of domestic reform in Turkey and to increasing strains in Turkey's relations with the EU. In effect, Turkish-EU relations can be roughly divided into two distinct phases. The first phase—what Ziya Önis has termed the "Golden Age of Europeanization in Turkey"[9]—

---

[9]   Ziya Öniş, "Turkey-EU Relations: Beyond the Current Stalemate," *Insight Turkey*, Vol. 10, No. 4, 2008, p. 40.

extended from late 2002 to the end of 2005. During this phase, the AKP built on the foundations laid by the previous coalition (headed by Bülent Ecevit) and pushed through a series of important economic and political reforms that paved the way for the EU's decision in December 2004 to open accession negotiations with Turkey.

The second phase, which began in late 2005, has been characterized by a loss of enthusiasm for and commitment to EU membership on Turkey's part and by a visible slowdown in Turkey's reform process. As Kivanç Ulusoy has argued, this slowdown is in large part due to the EU's negotiating strategy.[10] The lack of a clear timetable and membership perspective, the promotion by Sarkozy and Merkel of the idea of a privileged partnership as an alternative to membership, and the failure of the EU to end the isolation of the TRNC after the northern Cypriots—with the strong encouragement and support of Ankara—voted for the Annan plan contributed to a loss in popular support for EU membership and a slowdown in the process of domestic reform.

The prospect of EU membership provided an important incentive for the AKP's reform efforts in 2002–2005. However, as the perception that membership was possible began to weaken in Turkey after 2005, so did the incentive for the AKP to give domestic reform a high priority. Turkey was expected to take bold steps toward reform. But as Ulusoy notes, it is extremely difficult to take bold steps unless those steps are complemented and supported by the EU. The Turkish government's political will for reform requires positive signals from the EU side and concrete deliverables if it is to be sustained.[11]

The slowdown in domestic reform since 2005 has resulted in increasing strains in Turkey's relations with the EU. Strains in Turkey's relations with the EU are, of course, nothing new: Turkish-EU relations have witnessed several periods of strain in the last several decades. However, in the past, when relations with the EU were bad, Turkey could always turn to the United States. But for the first time in the

---

[10] Kivanç Ulusoy, "Turkey and the EU: Democratization, Civil-Military Relations and the Cyprus Issue," *Insight Turkey*, Vol. 10, No. 4, 2008, pp. 51–76.

[11] Ulusoy, 2008, p. 66.

past two decades, Turkey's relations with both Europe and the United States are strained at the same time.

This simultaneous deterioration of relations with the United States and the EU has contributed to a growing sense of vulnerability and nationalism in Turkey. An increasing number of Turks feel that Turkey can no longer rely on its traditional allies, especially the United States.[12] This has reinforced a kind of siege mentality and resulted in a growing sense of suspicion and mistrust of the West within large parts of the Turkish elite. As Barkey, one of the most respected Turkey watchers in the United States, has observed, today, many Turks "are wallowing in fear and self-doubt, suspecting anybody and everybody—indeed the world at large—of ganging up on them."[13]

This does not mean that Turkey is about to turn its back on the West. Ankara remains strongly embedded in a Western framework. But more and more Turks are feeling disenchanted with and abandoned by the West. If the current strains in Turkey's relations with the EU continue to deepen, or if the door to EU membership is permanently closed to Turkey, Ankara could begin to pursue a more independent, nationalistic policy or seek to explore other strategic options more seriously. Such a development would have important strategic consequences for the United States and make many issues, from Cyprus to peace in the Middle East, more difficult to resolve.

Relations with Greece

One of the most important factors affecting Turkey's prospects for EU membership has been the change in Turkish relations with Greece. For

---

[12] According to a poll by the German Marshall Fund, nearly half of the Turkish respondents felt that Turkey should act alone on international matters. See Transatlantic Trends, 2008, p. 21. As Soli Özel has noted, this high degree of unilateralism reflects a perception in Turkey that the country's allies do not care much for Turkey's interests and do not keep their promises to help Turkey in matters that it considers to be vital to its security. See Soli Özel, "Will Turkey Opt Out?" *On Turkey*, German Marshall Fund of the United States, September 15, 2008a, p. 2.

[13] Henri J. Barkey, "Notes from a Funeral," *The American Interest*, July/August 2007b, p. 140.

much of the 1980s and 1990s, Turkish-Greek relations were tense and marred by conflict. In February 1996, the two countries nearly went to war over the islets of Imia/Kardak. A military conflict between the two NATO allies was avoided only at the last minute by active U.S. diplomatic intervention.

However, since 1999, relations between Greece and Turkey have significantly improved.[14] Today, bilateral relations are better than they have been since the Atatürk-Venizelos era in the 1930s. Trade has increased visibly, as have tourism and people-to-people exchanges. Energy cooperation has also intensified, bolstered by the opening of a $300-million gas pipeline that creates an energy corridor connecting the rich natural-gas fields in the Caucasus with Europe.

The improvement in Greek-Turkish relations has been facilitated by a significant shift in Greek policy toward Turkey's membership in the EU. For years, Greece sought to block Turkish membership in the EU in an effort to force changes in Turkish behavior favorable to Greek interests. Since 1999, however, Greece has become one of the strongest advocates of Turkey's EU membership. Today, Athens sees a "Europeanized" Turkey as strongly in its own interest. From the Greek perspective, the more Turkey conforms with European norms and standards of international behavior, the better Greek-Turkish relations are likely to be.

This shift in Greek policy toward Turkey's EU membership has contributed to overall improvement in Greek-Turkish relations. However, there has been little progress in resolving differences over the Aegean, especially over air space. In the last several years, the number of violations and incidents has increased to a dangerous degree.[15] In

---

[14] For background on the origins of and initial impetus behind the rapprochement between Greece and Turkey since 1999, see Larrabee and Lesser, 2003, pp. 84–88.

[15] According to the TGS, Turkish aircraft were intercepted by Greek air forces 161 times during the first six months of 2009. This means that Greek and Turkish aircraft engage in dogfights on nearly a daily basis. For its part, Greece complains that the number of flights by Turkish aircraft over Greek-populated residential areas doubled in the first six months of 2009 compared with 2008. See Serkan Demirtas, "New Political Guidance Needed for Turkey-Greece Ties," *Hürriyet Daily News and Economic Review* (Istanbul), May 18, 2009. See also "Turkish, Greek Dogfights Cause of Concern in the Aegean," *Today's Zaman* (Istan-

2006, a Greek pilot was killed when his F-16 collided with a Turkish jet in an area where dogfights between Greek and Turkish aircraft often take place. This incident highlighted the dangers of leaving the outstanding differences over the Aegean unresolved. As long as these issues remain unresolved, there is a danger that an incident could escalate and lead to a military confrontation, as nearly happened in 1996 over the islets of Imia/Kardak.

At a time when NATO faces major challenges to its cohesion and mission in Afghanistan, the last thing the United States needs is a divisive new crisis in the Aegean. Moreover, the incidents have a corrosive effect on the overall tenor of bilateral relations, making other bilateral issues harder to resolve. If the problems in the Aegean are allowed to fester, it will be difficult to maintain the impetus behind the historic rapprochement between Turkey and Greece that has taken place since 1999.

Cyprus

The Turkish-Greek rapprochement in the last decade has reduced the saliency of the Cyprus issue as a source of friction in bilateral Turkish-Greek relations. Cyprus continues to be a problem, but the dynamics of the problem have changed in important ways. In the 1970s and 1980s, Cyprus was closely bound with Turkey's conflict with Greece and was seen, especially by the Turkish military, as important for the defense of Turkey's interests in the Eastern Mediterranean. With Turkey's rapprochement with Greece, however, Cyprus has receded as a potential flashpoint that could spark a conflict between the two countries.

Today, the prospects for a settlement of the Cyprus issue are influenced more heavily by the social and economic dynamic between the two Cypriot communities on the island than by the policies of Greece and Turkey. In effect, Cyprus has increasingly been decoupled from bilateral Turkish-Greek relations. At the same time, with the admis-

bul), June 15, 2009; "Greek FM Concerned About Rising Tension," *Hürriyet Daily News and Economic Review* (Istanbul), June 24, 2009.

sion of the Republic of Cyprus into the EU in May 2004, the Cyprus issue has become closely bound up with Turkey's EU candidacy. Today, Cyprus is important as a complicating factor in Turkey's relations with the EU rather than as a potential flashpoint that could unleash a Turkish-Greek military conflict.

Under the Customs Union agreement it signed with the EU in 1996, Turkey is obligated to open its ports and airports to Cypriot vessels and aircraft now that Cyprus is a full member of the EU. However, Turkey has refused to do so until the EU fulfills its promise to lift its trade embargo against the TRNC. In response, the EU Council voted in December 2006 to suspend eight out of 35 chapters in the accession negotiation. Ankara faces a deadline at the end of 2009 to implement the agreed protocol governing the access of Greek Cypriot ships and aircraft to Turkish ports. If Turkey fails to implement the protocol, the EU could freeze more chapters in the accession negotiations and possibly even suspend the negotiations entirely.

A Cyprus settlement would give Turkey's membership bid an important boost. However, prospects for an early settlement are dim. The strong showing of the right-wing National Unity Party, which garnered 44 percent of the vote in the parliamentary elections in northern Cyprus in April 2009, has sharpened divisions within the Turkish Cypriot community and weakened the ability of Turkish Cypriot leader Mehmet Ali Talat, the leader of the ruling Republican Turkish party, to negotiate a settlement. Thus, a major breakthrough in the talks seems unlikely in the near future.

The Uncertain Outlook

Cyprus complicates Turkey's relations with the EU, but the most serious obstacle to Turkish membership in the EU is the pace of internal reform in Turkey. Although the Erdoğan government continues to assert that EU membership is an important strategic priority, the process of domestic reform in areas of concern to the EU has visibly slowed since 2005. Some steps have been taken to modify the controversial Article 301 of the Turkish penal code and to protect the rights of non-Muslim minorities, but these measures have been implemented in a defensive and half-hearted manner. As a result, Turkey's membership bid has lost valuable momentum.

Given the growing anti-EU sentiment in Turkey, the Erdoğan government feels little pressure to revitalize the EU-accession process. Indeed, being perceived as too pro-EU is a political liability in Turkey's current political climate. Membership remains an important long-term goal, but Turkish officials today stress that Turkey is "not in any rush" to join the EU.[16] Accession negotiations are likely to limp along, more out of inertia than enthusiasm on either side. But without a greater commitment to domestic reform in Ankara, Turkey's membership prospects will remain problematic.

A lot will depend on the evolution of the EU. If the EU evolves into a looser, more flexible intergovernmental organization—along the lines of the British model, which allows for significant national autonomy—Turkish accession could be easier. By contrast, if the French model, which features closer and deeper integration, prevails, Turkey's accession will be more difficult, increasing Ankara's growing sense of alienation and exclusion.

Another possibility is phased membership. Under this scheme, Turkey would be integrated into the EU in stages, beginning with one or two concrete areas, such as foreign and security policy. Later, other areas, such as economics and justice, could be added. This approach would stretch out the accession process and give Turkey more time to prepare for membership. It would keep Turkey closely anchored to Europe while still keeping open the possibility of full membership in the future, thereby avoiding the overtones of discrimination or second-class citizenship implied in the privileged-partnership concept advocated by Sarkozy and other European leaders.

---

[16] See President Gül's interview in the German weekly *Der Spiegel* in "We're Not in Any Rush to Join the EU," *Spiegel Online*, October 20, 2008.

CHAPTER SEVEN

U.S.-Turkish Defense Cooperation

The general downturn in U.S.-Turkish relations has been reflected in defense and defense-industrial cooperation. In recent years, U.S. defense cooperation with Turkey has been marred by significant difficulties. Congress has held up a number of major weapon sales to Turkey due to Turkey's human rights policy and its policy toward Cyprus. These delays have had a damaging impact on U.S.-Turkish defense cooperation. As a result, Turkey has begun to expand its defense relationships with other nations that have fewer procurement restrictions, particularly Israel and Russia.

The U.S.-Turkish defense-industry relationship has two aspects: government-to-government purchases based on foreign-military sales and commercial sales in which U.S. firms have to compete with foreign rivals. The government-to-government sales have continued to develop reasonably well. Turkey is set to buy new fighter aircraft and related services worth $15 billion over the next 10–15 years, including 100 F-35 Joint Strike Fighters, 30 F-16s, and the modernization of older Turkish F-16s.[1]

Commercial sales, however, have been declining. Until Sikorsky finalized a sale of 17 Seahawk helicopters in the fall of 2006, no U.S. firm had won a major direct commercial sale since 2002.[2] Since 2006,

---

[1] Ümit Enginsoy and Burak Ege Bekdil, "Turkey Increasingly Shuns US Weapons," *Defense News*, July 7, 2007b.

[2] See "Testimony for Mr. Daniel Fata, Deputy Assistant Secretary for Europe and NATO, U.S. House of Representatives House Committee on Foreign Affairs," *Insight Turkey*, Vol. 9, No. 1, 2007, p. 36.

Turkey decided to conclude a $2.7-billion deal with the Italian-British firm Augusta Westland for attack helicopters, and it has also decided to buy trainer aircraft and main battle tanks from South Korean firms. Many U.S. companies failed to bid on these projects, complaining that Turkish terms were not compatible with U.S. export requirements.

Some of the problems in the defense-industry relationship—particularly delays due to Congress's concerns about Turkey's human rights record—have been on the U.S. side. Strict U.S. restrictions on technology transfer have also caused the Turks to shun U.S. weapon systems and turn to non-U.S. manufacturers, such as Israel and South Korea.

There have been problems on the Turkish side as well. Turkish defense programs often have an unrealistically ambitious scope. As a result, during competition, the programs are often scaled back, causing delays in the procurement process and frustration to U.S. contractors who have to revise their bids, often several times. In addition, the Turks often make unrealistic demands for technology transfers, causing major delays. U.S. contractors also complain about a lack of coordination between end-users and the procurement office.

As a result, Turkey has earned a reputation as a difficult and unpredictable client. U.S. contractors, exhausted after investing large amounts of resources, time, and effort, often find that the initial parameters and rules have been changed in midstream. In May 2004, for instance, Turkey shelved a $4-billion tank coproduction plan and halted $3 billion in attack-helicopter and aerial-vehicle projects. Decisions like this have made U.S. contractors very skittish about bidding on Turkish programs.

Turkey has also stepped up efforts to meet more of its defense needs through acquisitions from local manufacturers. In December 2007, Turkish Defense Minister Vecdi Gönül announced that, for the first time, Turkey would develop its own infantry rifles and automatic rifles.[3] Gönül also announced that Turkey would build four frigates that would be entirely produced in Turkish shipyards. Today, Turkey's

---

[3]   Gareth Jenkins, "Turkey Trying to Go Local in Defense Procurement," *Eurasia Daily Monitor*, Vol. 4, No. 226, December 6, 2007b.

defense industry receives about 25 percent of the military's annual procurement spending.[4] Current plans call for Turkey to purchase 50 percent of its defense needs locally by 2010.[5]

However, Turkey has a long way to go before its defense industry-has a serious impact on the Turkish economy. Moreover, there is a lack of strong civilian oversight over the defense budget and procurement process. The Parliamentary Planning and Budget Committee reviews the budget of the Defense Ministry. However, extrabudgetary funds are excluded from parliamentary scrutiny. The Defense Industry Support Fund, the mechanism through which most procurement projects are funded, is an extrabudgetary fund.

Priority in the defense budget is still put on acquiring weapons and such equipment as fighter aircraft, modern submarines, and tanks designed to defend against conventional threats. However, the terrorist threat posed by the PKK has created growing pressure for more funds to combat asymmetric threats. The continued supply of U.S. electronic intelligence is particularly important and has enabled Turkish fighter aircraft to launch strikes on PKK positions deep inside northern Iraq.

In addition, Turkey is looking to buy AH-1W Super Cobra attack helicopters and sophisticated Reaper drones.[6] The two weapon systems are regarded by the Turkish military as high-priority items in the struggle against the PKK. Turkey signed a contract with the Italian-British firm AgustaWestland for coproduction of at least 50 T129 gunships in 2008, but the systems are not expected to be available before late 2013, at best. Thus, the Super Cobras and Reaper drones represent a stopgap measure until the T129s come on line.

---

[4] Ümit Enginsoy and Burak Ege Bekdil, "Amid Squabbles, Turkish Military, Civilians Agree to Buy Locally," *Defense News*, September 10, 2007d.

[5] Tutku Ayvaz, "Turk Defense Industry Makes Strides," *Turkish Daily News* (Istanbul), December 27, 2007.

[6] Ümit Enginsoy and Burak Ege Bekdil, "U.S., Turkey Work on Super Cobra Sale," *Defense News*, June 15, 2009b; "Turkey to Buy Weapons from US," *Hurriyet Daily News and Economic Review* (Istanbul), June 24, 2009.

Military-to-Military Cooperation

Bilateral military-to-military cooperation has weakened since the end of the Cold War. Part of the reason for the weakening is attributable to the disappearance of the Soviet threat. This has resulted in significant decrease in the U.S. military presence in Turkey, which has declined from 15,000 in the late 1980s to around 2,000 personnel today.

A second reason is related to the two countries' different defense and national-security priorities. The Turkish military is focused on combating internal enemies, particularly the PKK and radical Islam, whereas the United States puts high priority on power projection and the global war on terrorism.

The U.S. invasion of Iraq in 2003 also contributed to a serious deterioration of military cooperation and military-to-military contacts. The Turkish Grand National Assembly's March 1, 2003, refusal to allow the U.S. Fourth Infantry Division to use Turkish territory to open a second front against Iraq left a sour taste in the mouths of many U.S. military personnel, who regarded the refusal as a sharp rebuff from a disloyal ally. They were therefore not very sympathetic to Turkish calls for help in fighting the PKK, having felt abandoned by the Turks when they needed Turkish assistance at the outset of the Iraq invasion.

These feelings of suspicion and mistrust were compounded by differences over how to deal with the Kurds in northern Iraq. The Turkish military regarded the Kurds with suspicion and hostility—literally as enemies—whereas the U.S. military viewed the Kurds as allies in the war against Saddam Hussein and the insurgency that emerged after Saddam's overthrow. The U.S. decision to decline Turkey's offer to send 10,000 Turkish troops to Iraq as members of the coalition—a decision largely made to avoid antagonizing the Kurds—was regarded by many Turkish officers as a strong rebuff, and it essentially froze Turkey out of any postwar planning in Iraq.

The failure of the United States to assist Turkey in the latter's struggle against the PKK had a particularly negative impact on military-to-military relations. The Turkish military regarded the struggle against the PKK as a major national-security priority and as the litmus test of the value of the U.S.-Turkish security partnership. Many

Turkish officers saw the U.S. refusal to assist Turkey as tantamount to siding with the Kurds against Turkey. The U.S. inaction resulted in growing bitterness and anti-American sentiment in the Turkish officer corps, particularly among younger officers who had not experienced the strong bonds between the U.S. and Turkish militaries forged by the struggle against the common Soviet threat during the Cold War.

The shift in the U.S. position regarding the PKK since Erdoğan's visit to Washington in November 2007—especially Washington's willingness to provide actionable intelligence—has contributed to closer military cooperation and an improvement in the overall atmosphere between the two militaries, as has the appointment of Başbuğ, who replaced Büyükanıt as chief of the TGS in August 2008. Başbuğ has made it clear that he regards strong links to NATO and the United States as essential to safeguarding Turkey's national security.

Under Başbuğ's leadership, military-to-military contacts between Turkey and the United States have begun to improve. But many obstacles continue to inhibit cooperation. Some are related to military culture and leadership. The TGS has a rigid, top-down system of command with little civilian control. It regards itself as the ultimate guarantor of Turkey's external *and internal* security. This internal-security function differentiates the Turkish military from other Western militaries and is used to legitimate its intervention in Turkish political life to a degree that goes beyond what is regarded as acceptable in Western democracies.

The quality of military-to-military interaction between the United States and Turkey, however, varies from service to service. The United States cooperates most closely with the Turkish Air Force, which is the most modern and outward-looking service. The Turkish Navy is focused on the Black Sea and the Aegean. Most U.S.-military interaction with the Turkish Navy occurs only during NATO exercises and operations.[7]

---

[7] See Stephen J. Flanagan and Samuel J. Brannen, *Turkey's Evolving Dynamics: Strategic Choices for U.S.-Turkey Relations*, Washington, D.C.: Center for Strategic & International Studies, 2009, p. 85.

There is very little interaction between the U.S. Army and the Turkish Land Forces, which is the largest but least-modernized service and the one least exposed to foreign-military contact and cultures. It is also the most powerful military service. Most of the top leadership positions in the TGS are held by generals from the Land Forces.

Some progress has recently been made in increasing U.S.-military cooperation with the Land Forces. The first-ever discussions between the U.S. Army Staff and the TGS took place in January 2009. Special-operations exercises were also resumed in 2008 after a six-year hiatus.[8] However, the level of cooperation between the U.S. Army and the Land Forces remains considerably below what it should be, particularly given the dominant role the Land Forces play in the TGS.

Use of Turkish Bases and Facilities

Another important source of strain has been U.S. access to Turkish bases and facilities. In recent years, the United States has faced increasing restrictions on its ability to conduct operations out of İncirlik Air Base. Although Turkey has allowed the United States to use İncirlik to transport personnel and materiel to Afghanistan and Iraq, it has refused to permit the United States to permanently station combat aircraft there or to use the base to fly combat missions in the Middle East or Persian Gulf region.[9] Thus, in the future, the United States cannot automatically assume that it can use İncirlik for purposes beyond those spelled out in the 1980 Defense and Economic Cooperation Agreement, particularly combat missions in the Middle East.

---

[8]   Flanagan and Brannen, 2009, p. 86.

[9]   As part of its Defense Posture Review, the Bush administration explored transferring 72 F-16s based in Spangdahlem, Germany, to İncirlik. However, the Erdoğan government opposed any permanent deployment of the aircraft at İncirlik and was unwilling to expand cooperation beyond the level and scope agreed to in the 1980 Defense and Economic Cooperation Agreement. See "US Considers Shifting New F-16s to Incirlik, Report Says," *Turkish Daily News* (Istanbul), June 5, 2004. See also "US: No Letup in Efforts for Broader Use of Incirlik," *Turkish Daily News* (Istanbul), August 18, 2007.

To hedge against a serious deterioration of U.S.-Turkish relations that could result in severe constraints on the use of Turkish bases or denial of their use altogether, the United States could gradually reduce its military presence in Turkey and conduct some of the missions currently carried out in Turkey from other friendly or allied countries in the region, such as Kuwait or Qatar. Doing so could have several benefits. It could reduce popular Turkish resentment against the U.S. military presence and diminish anti-Americanism in Turkey, while still allowing the United States to continue to carry out most of the current missions being performed at İncirlik and other facilities in Turkey. Such a move could be portrayed as an adjustment to the new security requirement arising after the end of the Cold War and as part of the overall Global Posture Review initiated by the Bush administration.

The success of this policy, however, would depend in part on the willingness of key allies, such as Kuwait and Qatar, to allow the United States to carry out new missions from their soil. Moreover, bases in these countries may not serve as substitutes for all of the functions currently provided by bases in Turkey. Hence, a switch would presumably lead to some loss of operational capability or efficiency, at least initially.

A second option is to station forces in northern Iraq. This option would allow the United States to maintain a foothold in the region and enable it to conduct from northern Iraq many of the missions it currently conducts from bases in Turkey.

However, this option has a number of significant downsides. First, unless the KRG were to take visible, concrete action to eliminate the PKK threat and resolve its differences with Turkey, the establishment of an expanded or permanent U.S. military presence in northern Iraq would severely strain U.S.-Turkish relations and could provoke strong retaliatory measures by Turkey (e.g., restrictions on the use of İncirlik Air Base and other Turkish facilities). Second, it could prompt Ankara to strengthen cooperation with Tehran and Damascus, both of which have Kurdish minorities on their soil and share Ankara's concerns about any moves that would strengthen Kurdish nationalism and encourage the emergence of an independent Kurdish state. Third, the United

States could find itself increasingly drawn into a dangerous regional dispute with Turkey, Iran, and Syria. This could have a spillover effect and make efforts to resolve other regional issues, especially the nuclear issue with Iran, more difficult, even impossible. Finally, stationing U.S. forces in northern Iraq could exacerbate U.S. relations with the Sunni Arabs and the Shia in Iraq.

Maritime Cooperation in the Black Sea

Efforts by the United States to promote increased maritime cooperation in the Black Sea need to take into consideration Turkey's strong historical and strategic interests in the Black Sea. Ankara essentially regards the Black Sea as a "Turkish lake" and opposes an expansion of either the NATO or the U.S. military presence there. Turkey blocked a U.S. initiative designed to increase the role of NATO's Operation Active Endeavor in the Black Sea.[10] The NATO initiative conflicted with Operation Black Sea Harmony, an initiative launched by the Turkish Navy in March 2004.

In addition, Turkey feared that an increased U.S. or NATO military presence in the Black Sea could exacerbate tensions with Russia. Turkish officials argue that Black Sea security should be provided by the littoral countries of the Black Sea. Instead of increasing the U.S. or NATO military presence, Turkey has proposed expanding the Black Sea Naval Cooperation Task Force (known as Blackseafor), a multinational naval task force that includes Russia, Ukraine, Georgia, Romania, and Bulgaria.[11]

Turkey also worried that the NATO initiative could lead to the erosion of the 1936 Montreux Convention, which regulates access to the Bosporus and Dardanelles. The convention is a cornerstone of Turkish foreign policy. Ankara is strongly opposed to any initiative

---

[10] Ümit Enginsoy and Burak Ege Bekdil, "Turks Oppose US Black Sea Move," *Defense News*, March 13, 2006.

[11] Serkan Demirtas, "Blackseafor to Be Expanded," *Turkish Daily News* (Istanbul), September 19, 2008.

that might imply a change in the status of the convention or that could disturb the maritime status quo in the Black Sea region.[12] Thus, any future proposals or initiatives for increased U.S.-Turkish cooperation in the Black Sea will need to take into consideration Turkey's acute sensitivity regarding changes in the maritime status quo in the region.

The NATO Connection

The difficulties noted above have taken place against the backdrop of growing Turkish unease about the directions of some aspects of NATO's transformation. During the Cold War, Turkish public support for Turkish membership in NATO was strong. Membership in the alliance was seen as an important guarantee of Turkey's security. In recent years, however, Turkish public support for NATO has visibly declined. According to a survey conducted by the German Marshall Fund of the United States, 53 percent of Turks polled in 2004 felt that NATO was essential to Turkish security; in 2007, only 35 percent felt that way.[13]

Some of this erosion of public support for NATO may be attributable to the end of the Cold War and Turkey's improved relations with Russia. The disappearance of the Soviet threat and the improvement in Ankara's ties to Moscow have made Turkey more cautious about irri-

---

[12] Turkish sensitivity about strictly abiding by provisions of the Montreux Convention was underscored in August 2008 in the immediate aftermath of the Russian invasion of Georgia. The United States sought to send two U.S. Navy hospital ships, the USNS *Comfort* and the USNS *Mercy*, through the Dardanelles with humanitarian aid for Georgia. Their tonnage, however, exceeded the limits allowed for foreign warships under the Montreux Convention. Turkey let it be known that the ships would not be allowed to pass through the Bosphorus because they violated the Montreux Convention. The United States eventually sent the aid aboard the destroyer USS *McFaul*, the USCGC *Dallas*, and the USS *Mount Whitney*, all of which were well below the tonnage limits allowed under the Montreux Convention. See Ümit Enginsoy and Burak Ege Bekdil, "Turkey Jealously Defends Its Rights on the Black Sea," *Defense News*, September 29, 2008b. On the United States' denial that it wanted a change in the Montreux Convention, see Ümit Enginsoy, "No Change Wanted on Turk Straits Convention," *Turkish Daily News* (Istanbul), August 28, 2008.

[13] See Transatlantic Trends, 2007, p. 22.

tating Moscow. Turkey has strong reservations about the enlargement of NATO to include Georgia and Ukraine, fearing that this could lead to an escalation of tension between NATO and Russia. As noted earlier, a serious deterioration of the West's relations with Moscow would make it much harder for Ankara to pursue a diversified foreign policy aimed at expanding its regional ties.

However, a large part of the decline in public support appears to reflect disenchantment with U.S. and European policy more broadly. The recent strains in Turkey's relations with the United States and the EU have led to a growing sense that Turkey cannot count on its traditional allies and must rely on its own devices to ensure its security. This feeling was strengthened by the initial reluctance of some NATO allies to respond positively to Turkey's requests in 1991 and 2003 that NATO deploy early warning systems and Patriot missiles to Turkish territory to counter the possibility of an Iraqi attack. This hesitation raised doubts in the minds of many Turks about whether Turkey could really rely on NATO in case of an outside attack.

Similarly, Turkey has viewed the reduced emphasis within the alliance on Article V of the Washington Treaty (the collective-defense provision) with unease. Turkey lives in a volatile neighborhood and is one of the few countries in NATO that face a serious possibility of conflict. Thus, Ankara does not want to see any weakening of the alliance's emphasis on collective defense. In addition, Turkey's differences with the EU over Cyprus have spilled over into the NATO arena, complicating NATO-EU cooperation.

Turkey's initial effort to block the selection of Danish Prime Minister Anders Fogh Rasmussen as NATO Secretary General because of Rasmussen's role in the widely publicized Islamic cartoon crisis in 2006 angered many European NATO members and left a sour aftertaste both in Brussels and in Ankara. Although Turkey eventually dropped its objection after the personal intervention of President Obama at the NATO summit in Kehl-Strasbourg in return for promises of receiving several top NATO posts, Rasmussen's selection was seen by many Turks as another sign of the alliance's unwillingness to take Turkish views and interests into consideration.

This is not to suggest that Turkey is about to leave NATO. Support for NATO within the Turkish political and military elite remains firm. However, the decline in public support for the alliance is troubling and bears close monitoring. If this support continues to erode, it could become a more serious political problem, one that could begin to affect Turkey's overall foreign-policy orientation.

Keeping Turkey firmly anchored in NATO is important. NATO membership provides a crucial means of ensuring Turkey's continued Western orientation, especially at a time when Ankara's relations with the EU are shaky and could become even shakier. Turkey's membership in NATO also represents an important hedge against any Turkish attempt to develop its own nuclear deterrent. Thus, ensuring that Turkey remains firmly embedded in NATO is strongly in the U.S. interest.

CHAPTER EIGHT
The Domestic Context

The strains in Turkey's relations with the West are all the more worrisome because they come at a time of growing internal stress and political polarization in Turkey. The country is going through a period of disruptive internal change that is testing many of the basic tenets of the Kemalist revolution on which the Turkish Republic was founded, particularly secularism. Kemalism still remains an important social and political force in Turkey. However, the democratization of Turkish political life in the last several decades has led to the emergence of new political and social elites that have increasingly begun to challenge the Kemalist elite's traditional dominance of Turkish political life. Public opinion also plays a much more important role today than it did a few decades ago. This has resulted in a much more diverse domestic and foreign policy debate and has made it much more difficult for the Kemalist elite to control the debate. It has also led to growing internal polarization and instability.

Religion and Identity

Secularism has been one of the key principles of the Kemalist revolution. However, in the last several decades, the strength of religion in Turkey has visibly increased. A study undertaken in 2006 by the Turkish Economic and Social Studies Foundation (TESEV) revealed a sharp increase in the number of Turks who identified themselves primarily as

Muslims (44.6 percent) and only secondarily as Turks (19.4 percent).[1] This suggests that Muslim identity has begun to play a stronger role in Turks' views of themselves and their place in the world.

The headscarf controversy has been an important reflection of the growing role of religion in Turkish life. For many religious-minded Turks, especially AKP supporters, wearing the headscarf is seen as a matter of personal choice. Turkish citizens, they believe, should be able to express their religious identity, even in state institutions. Secularists, however, regard the wearing of the headscarf in state institutions and universities—a practice that is banned under the Turkish constitution—as an assault on the very fabric of the secularist state in Turkey.

The controversy over the headscarf has become more acute since the assumption of power by the AKP, which has strong Islamic roots. The AKP's attempt to nominate Gül—whose wife wears a headscarf—as a candidate for president touched off a major political crisis in the spring of 2007. Secularists were willing to accept an AKP member as president in principle, but not one whose wife, who might appear with her husband at official state functions, wore a headscarf. This wearing of the headscarf at official functions was seen as a violation of the basic principles of secularism on which the Turkish Republic was founded.

These developments do not mean that Turkey is about to become "Iranized." Most Turks, even deeply religious ones, are strongly attached to secularism. The TESEV study found that 76 percent of the Turks polled opposed the implementation of shari'a and 9 percent favored it. This represented a substantial decline from the 26 percent who had favored the introduction of shari'a in 1996.[2]

Recent studies suggest, moreover, that religious conservatism is on the rise more in appearance than in reality. A survey by the Pew Research Center published in September 2008, for instance, revealed that although Turks have become more religious, only 20 percent

---

[1]   Ali Çarkoğlu and Binnaz Toprak, *Degisen Turkiye . . . 'de Din Toplum ve Slyaset*, Istanbul: Turkish Economic and Social Studies Foundation, in Turkish, 2006.

[2]   Çarkoğlu and Toprak, 2006.

fasted for all of Ramadan and only 34 percent prayed five times a day.[3] With rising levels of education and income, the study suggests, Turks have become more flexible and less conservative. The TESEV study, for instance, found that the number of women wearing the headscarf has actually declined in the last decade.[4]

Two factors explain this discrepancy between appearance and reality. First, as a result of urbanization, many pious women from rural areas have migrated to the cities. Thus, one sees many more women wearing headscarves today in Turkish cities than was the case a decade ago, even though the overall number of women wearing headscarves has actually declined. Second, as a result of the democratization and social transformation of Turkish society in the last several decades, many of the pious women who would have stayed at home and not been seen in public a decade ago now venture out to cafés and restaurants. Thus, women wearing headscarves are now more visible (though not more numerous) than a decade ago.

Kemalism Versus Neo-Ottomanism

To some extent, the current polarization reflects a tension between two contending ideologies or visions of Turkish identity: Kemalism and neo-Ottomanism. Kemalism has been the dominant ideology since the founding of the Turkish Republic in 1923. It is based on three main pillars: militant secularism, assimilative nationalism, and Westernization. However, in the last several decades, it has been increasingly challenged by the emergence of what has been termed *neo-Ottomanism*. Kemalism is based on a rejection of Turkey's Ottoman past in both domestic and foreign policy. Neo-Ottomanism, by contrast, sees positive elements in Turkey's Ottoman past and wants to draw on these elements to form a new synthesis in foreign and domestic policy.

---

[3] "Conservative But Relaxed About It," *Turkish Daily News* (Istanbul), September 20–21, 2008.

[4] Çarkoğlu and Toprak, 2006.

In terms of foreign policy, neo-Ottomanism is not anti-Western, but its adherents believe that Turkey's Western ties should be complemented by ties to other regions, particularly to those areas, such as the Middle East, where Turkey has long-standing historical interests and ties. It sees Turkey as a bridge linking a number of geographic areas where Ottoman power and influence were once strong: the Balkans, the Caucasus/Central Asia, and the Middle East. In domestic policy, it advocates a more inclusive and tolerant attitude toward religion and non-Turkish communities, especially the Kurds. Whereas Kemalism stresses assimilationist nationalism based on a strict definition of "Turkishness," neo-Ottomanism, in keeping with Ottoman traditions, is more open to multiculturalism.

Today, Turkey seems increasingly torn between these two identities. Kemalists, especially the military, are uncomfortable with neo-Ottomanism for three reasons. They fear it will (1) lead to a weakening of secularism and a strengthening of Islam in Turkish political life, (2) strengthen Kurdish nationalism and separatism and ultimately pose a threat to the territorial integrity of the Turkish state, and (3) weaken Turkey's ties to the West.

Yet this need not necessarily be the case. The best example that suggests that the two ideologies are compatible and can coexist is provided by former Turkish President Turgut Özal. A Western-trained technocrat who had worked for the World Bank, Özal was also a supporter of the Nakşibendi order and had been associated with Islamist National Salvation Party before founding the Motherland Party in 1983. He thus bridged the secular-Islamic divide. As Barkey has noted, "he was as comfortable with Western leaders as in a mosque."[5]

As president, Özal advocated a more open and tolerant attitude toward the Kurds and Islam, while in foreign policy, he sought to expand Turkey's ties to the Middle East and the Turkic nations of Central Asia. At the same time, he firmly backed the United States in the first Gulf War—against the advice and strong opposition of the military, who, as good Kemalists, believed Turkey should stay aloof from

---

[5] Henri J. Barkey, "The Struggles of a 'Strong' State," *Journal of International Affairs,* Vol. 54, No. 2, Fall 2000, p. 99.

involvement in Middle East conflicts—and also pushed aggressively for Turkish membership in the EC.

The Nature of the Kemalist Revolution

The cause of the current political polarization in Turkey has its roots in the nature of the Kemalist revolution. The Kemalist revolution was essentially a revolution from above. It was a state-instituted, top-down enterprise in social engineering carried out by a small, military-bureaucratic elite that imposed its secularist vision on a reluctant traditional society. In carrying out this transformation, little effort was made to co-opt or cajole the population or the opposition. Instead, the elite simply tried to use the "strong state" to overwhelm and intimidate any opposition.[6]

The new Kemalist elite sought a radical break with the Ottoman past. The Ottoman era and everything associated with it, except a few elements of past grandeur, were condemned and discarded in favor of a new project based on Westernization and secularism. However, the Kemalist revolution never really penetrated the countryside. Until the 1950s, the bulk of the Turkish population remained isolated and traditional, while the urban centers were modern and secular. In effect, two Turkeys coexisted in uneasy harmony: an urban, modern, and secular "center" and a rural, traditional, and religious "periphery,"[7] with little contact occurring between the two. The dominant elite were urban, modern, and secular, while the bulk of the population was rural, traditional, and pious.

Religion was not completely suppressed or eliminated, however. It was simply banished from the public sphere and strictly subordinated

---

[6] On the concept of the strong state and its use by the Kemalist elite in the modernization process, see in particular Barkey, 2000, pp. 87–105; Metin Heper, "The Problem of the Strong State for the Consolidation of Democracy," *Comparative Political Studies*, Vol. 25, July 1992.

[7] For a detailed discussion of the center-periphery dichotomy and its impact on Turkish politics, see Serif Mardin, "Center-Periphery Relations: A Key to Turkish Politics?" *Daedalus*, Vol. 102, No. 1, 1973, pp. 169–190.

to, and supervised by, the state through the Directorate of Religious Affairs. In effect, religious institutions became appendages of the state, with their personnel acting as civil servants. In the countryside, however, Islam continued to have strong social roots and remained largely beyond state control despite the ban on religious orders (organizations known as *tarikatlar*) introduced in 1925.

Indeed, a kind of religious counterculture existed outside the cities. In response to their forced exclusion from the political sphere, many Muslims established their own informal networks and educational systems. These religious networks and brotherhoods, such as the Nakşibendi and the Nurculuk movement, became a kind of counter–public sphere and the incubators of a more popular Islamic identity. Islam, as Hakan Yavuz has noted, remained the "hidden identity of the Kemalist state" and provided the vernacular for the marginalized majority excluded from the top-down transformation.[8]

Like its Ottoman predecessor, the Kemalist state discouraged the development of autonomous groups outside the control of the state. Autonomous activity, especially religious activity, was regarded by the state as a potential threat to its ability to carry out its modernization effort and consolidate its political control. Instances of dissent and opposition to the regime's nationalist ideology and modernization policies were quickly suppressed. This attempt to suppress expressions of autonomous activity outside the control of the state not only alienated the large majority of the rural population, for whom religion was an important part of daily life—it also hindered the development of civil society more generally.[9]

---

[8]   Hakan Yavuz, "Cleansing Islam from the Public Sphere," *Journal of International Affairs*, Vol. 54, No. 1, Fall 2000, pp. 21–42.

[9]   See Binnaz Toprak, "The State, Politics and Religion in Turkey," in Metin Heper and Ahmet Evin, eds., *State, Democracy and the Military: Turkey in the 1980s*, Berlin/New York: Walter de Gruyter, 1988, pp. 119–136.

Modernization, Social Change, and the Rise of Islam

The economic and political reforms carried out in the mid-1980s when Özal was prime minister greatly contributed to the growth of Islamic forces in Turkish political and social life. These reforms weakened the state's control over the economy and created a new class of entrepreneurs and capitalists in the provincial towns of Anatolia, such as Denizli, Gaziantep, and Kahramanmaraş. The economic upswing created a new middle class—the so-called Anatolian bourgeoisie—with strong roots in Islamic culture. This group favors liberal economic policies and a reduction of the role of the state in the economic and social spheres. It acts as an alternative—or parallel—elite to the secular business community in Istanbul and is one of the core constituencies backing the AKP.

Özal's reforms also opened up greater political space for new political groups, including the Islamists. Islamist groups gained access to important media outlets and newspaper chains, which allowed them to reach a much broader political audience.[10] Television in particular provided an important means of propagating the Islamists' message.[11]

Demographic changes also contributed to the strengthening of the role of Islam in Turkey. The industrial and modernization policies pursued by successive Turkish governments precipitated a large-scale influx of the rural population into the cities. These rural migrants brought with them traditional habits, beliefs, and customs. Uprooted and alienated, many lived in makeshift shanty towns (known as *gecekondu*) on the outskirts of large cities and were not integrated into urban culture. They represented an important pool of potential voters for Islamic parties opposed to Westernization and the forces of globalization.

---

[10] Serif Mardin has noted the important role played by the expansion of the media in propagating the Islamic voice and contributing to the rise of Islamic political parties. See Serif Mardin, "Turkish Islamic Exceptionalism, Yesterday and Today: Continuity, Rupture and Reconstruction in Operational Codes," *Journal of International Affairs*, Vol. 54, No. 1, Fall 2000, p. 157.

[11] Until 1989, Turkey had only one television channel, the state-run Turkish Radio and Television Corporation. The first religiously oriented television channels began to emerge in 1993 and were linked to the Gülen movement.

Ironically, the military also contributed to the strengthening of political Islam in Turkey. After the coup in September 1980, in an effort to combat communism and leftist ideologies, the military sought to strengthen the role of Islam. Under the military's tutelage, religious education was made a compulsory subject in all schools. Quranic classes were opened, and state-controlled moral and religious education was promoted.

In effect, the military sought to institute a process of state-controlled Islamization from above. By fusing Islamic symbols with nationalism, the military hoped to both create a more homogenous and less political Islamic community and insulate the population from the influence of left-wing ideologies. Based on the tripod of "the family, the mosque, and the barracks," this "Turkish-Islamic synthesis" was designed to reduce the appeal of radical leftist ideologies as and diminish the influence of non-Turkish strands of Islamic thinking from Pakistan and the Arab world.[12]

The new synthesis, however, sent an ambiguous message. On one hand, under the 1982 constitution, Turkey was defined as a secular state. On the other hand, the role of religion was strengthened in schools as a means of reinforcing Turkish nationalism. This tended to weaken the emphasis on secularism. At the same time, it provided opportunities for the Islamists to expand and reinforce their own message.

The Ideological Transformation of the Islamic Movement

In the last decade, the Islamic movement in Turkey has undergone an important evolution and ideological transformation.[13] Islamic political identity in Turkey traditionally was built in opposition to the West, which was regarded as an entity to be rejected or countered. The predecessors of the AKP, such as the National Salvation Party and Refah, were strongly anti-Western. They opposed Turkey's membership in

---

[12] Cemal Karakas, *Turkey: Islam and Laicism Between the Interests of the State, Politics and Society*, Report No. 78, Peace Research Institute Frankfurt (PIRF), 2007, pp. 17–18.

[13] For a detailed discussion, see Rabasa and Larrabee, 2008.

NATO and the EU and saw Turkey's salvation in closer ties to the Muslim world.

However, since its establishment in August 2001, the AKP has increasingly begun to emphasize Western political values, such as democracy, respect for human rights, and rule of law, in its public discourse. At the same time, the party has come to view the West, and especially the EU, as an important ally in its struggle against the restrictions of the Kemalist state. Whereas Islamists in Turkey formerly regarded Western calls for greater democratic reform as an attempt to impose alien values on Turkish society, the AKP sees the Western agenda increasingly overlapping with its own. The party views membership in the EU as a means of reducing the influence of the military and establishing a political framework that will expand religious tolerance and ensure its own political survival.

The jettisoning of anti-Western rhetoric has been accompanied by an abandonment of the antiglobalization discourse that characterized the Islamist movement in the past. The 2001 economic crisis made clear to Ankara that strictly adhering to the program of the International Monetary Fund and attracting more foreign investment were indispensable to overcoming Turkey's financial difficulties and putting the Turkish economy back on its feet. Thus, the AKP has promoted liberal market policies designed to attract foreign investment and integrate Turkey more closely into the global economy.

The AKP's ideological makeover and transformation have helped the party expand its political base and contributed to its electoral success. Although the AKP has Islamic roots, it enjoys broad-based political support that transcends religious, class, and regional differences. Its widespread social networks and efficient party machine, which has close ties to local constituencies, have allowed it to gain strong support among the poor and marginalized groups—many of them pious and socially conservative—that make up a growing portion of Turkey's urban areas.

At the same time, the party's liberal, free-market economic policies attract the provincial entrepreneurial classes in Anatolia—the so-called Anatolian tigers—that are socially conservative but integrated into the global economy. Finally, the AKP's support for democratic reform and its tolerant policy toward minorities have enabled it to obtain the support of many Kurds, Alevis, and Armenians. In short, the AKP enjoys broad social support; it is not a narrow, religion-based party.

The results of the July 22, 2007, election illustrate the degree to which the AKP has been able to expand its base of support. In the election, the AKP increased its electoral support in all seven regions of the country. The most important increases occurred in the predominantly Kurdish areas of southeastern Anatolia. The AKP also increased its support in the five largest cities in Turkey. In Istanbul, it received almost as many votes as all its opponents combined. In effect, as Tanju Tosun has argued, the AKP has become a "catchall party" and cannot be regarded as simply a religious party.[14]

Growing Internal Polarization

During its first few years in power, the AKP pursued a broadly reformist agenda and generally refrained from taking controversial measures that could antagonize the Kemalist establishment.[15] However, internal tensions between the AKP and the Kemalist establishment, especially the military, have intensified since 2007.

Two developments in particular contributed to an escalation of social tensions. The first was Erdoğan's decision to nominate Gül, the foreign minister at the time, as the AKP's candidate for president in the spring of 2007. The presidency had traditionally been held by a secularist. Gül's election would have allowed the AKP to hold all three key levers of political power in Turkey: the positions of the Prime Minister, the President, and the Speaker of Parliament. Kemalists feared that the AKP would use its strengthened power to change the Turkish constitution in ways that would weaken secularism and gradually move Turkey in a more Islamist direction.

---

[14] Tanju Tosun, "The July 22 Elections: A Chart for the Future of Turkish Politics," *Private View*, No. 12, Autumn 2007, p. 54.

[15] For a detailed discussion, see Rabasa and Larrabee, 2008, Chapter Four.

The decision to nominate Gül sparked large-scale public demonstrations by the supporters of secularism and prompted a blunt warning posted on the Web site of the TGS—a warning often referred to as the *e-memorandum* or the *midnight memorandum*—declaring that the military was "the definite defender of secularism" and would "manifest its attitude and behavior in an explicit and clear fashion when necessary."[16] This message was seen by many Turks as a veiled threat of a possible military coup.

The military's veiled threat backfired, however. In the parliamentary elections held on July 22, 2007, the AKP won an overwhelming victory, winning 46.6 percent of the vote—12 percent more than the party obtained in the 2002 elections. This decisive AKP victory strengthened Erdoğan's hand in his battle with the military. Emboldened by the strong electoral victory, Erdoğan submitted Gül's nomination for the presidency, and Gül was elected president on August 28, 2007.

Gül's election marked an important watershed in Turkish politics. For the first time in the history of the Turkish Republic, a nonsecularist had been elected president. This broke an important political tradition and gave the AKP control of all three key political posts. At the same time, it destroyed the political equilibrium within the AKP leadership. Gül had acted as a balancing factor within the leadership. Gül's elevation to the presidency removed an important constraint on Erdoğan's freedom of action. Since Gül's assumption of the presidency, Erdoğan has shown signs of increasing unilateralist and authoritarian tendencies. These tendencies have provoked growing criticism and contributed to a decline in support for the AKP, particularly among the urban middle class.

The second catalyst for the escalation of social tensions was Erdoğan's decision in late fall 2007 to press for a lifting of the ban on the wearing of the headscarf by women in universities. This move was seen by the secular establishment, especially the military, as a direct assault on the principle of secularism and a step toward the increased Islamization of Turkish society. The decision also came as a surprise

---

[16] Turkish General Staff, press release, April 27, 2007.

because during the initial period after the July 2007 election, Erdoğan had adopted a conciliatory approach, indicating that his government would press for greater democracy, rejuvenate Turkey's EU membership bid, and concentrate on constitutional reform.

It is unclear why Erdoğan decided to depart from this moderate approach. The most likely explanation, as İlter Turan has suggested, is that when the head of the National Action Party, Detlev Bahceli, suggested that it was possible to lift the headscarf ban if Erdoğan was really serious about wanting to do it, Erdoğan felt that he had to accept the challenge.[17]

Whatever the motivation for his action, Erdoğan's decision to lift the headscarf ban proved to be a serious strategic mistake. It provoked a strong reaction among Kemalists, who believed that the move crossed a political redline, and sparked one of the most serious political crises in Turkey's postwar history. On March 14, 2008, the public prosecutor forwarded a 162-page indictment to the Constitutional Court calling for the closure of the AKP and the banning of 71 AKP members—including Erdoğan and Gül—from politics for five years. The indictment accused the AKP leadership of violating the principles of secularism as defined in Article 2 of the Turkish constitution.

Although the Constitutional Court decided at the end of July 2008 to fine the AKP rather than shut it down, the AKP was forced on the defensive by the indictment and, for five months, was preoccupied with fighting for its political survival. As a consequence, domestic-reform plans and other important priorities were relegated to the backburner and lost critical political momentum. Erdoğan's credibility and reputation as a prudent political leader were also damaged by his decision to repeal the headscarf ban rather than focusing on reforming the constitution and revitalizing Turkey's EU-membership bid, which he had originally indicated would be his top priorities.

---

[17] İlter Turan, "War at Home, Peace Abroad!" *Private View*, No. 13, Autumn 2008, p. 8.

The March 2009 Municipal Elections

The AKP's first term in office was marked by a strong commitment to internal reform. This commitment to domestic reform was an important reason for the party's electoral success and ability to expand its political base in the elections in 2002 and 2007. However, since its electoral victory in July 2007, the AKP's commitment to reform has visibly weakened, and the Erdoğan government has pursued policies aimed at maintaining the political status quo. Turkey's EU-membership bid has stalled. The AKP also initially adopted a more nationalistic stance toward the Kurdish issue.[18] The party's image has been tarnished by charges of corruption.

As a consequence, popular support for the AKP has declined. The party suffered a sharp setback in the municipal elections in March 2009. Although it received 39 percent of the vote, well ahead of the runner-up (the secularist CHP, which obtained 23 percent of the vote), this was a significant drop from the 47 percent that it obtained in the July 2007 national elections. The AKP lost 12 cities, including such important cities as Adana and Antalya, and did poorly in the predominantly Kurdish areas of the southeast, where it had scored heavily in 2007.

The AKP did well in the conservative working-class districts (*varos*) in the major cities. However, it suffered a significant loss of support among the middle class in major cities, such as Istanbul, Ankara, and Izmir.[19] To a large extent, these losses were attributable to the slowdown in the democratization process and to the AKP's pursuit of polarizing policies, such as its attempt to repeal the headscarf law, which alienated the urban middle classes. The party was also hurt by the decline in the economy that resulted from the global economic crisis.

---

[18] See "U-Turn in AKP's Kurdish Policy," *Hürriyet Daily News and Economic Review* (Istanbul), November 10, 2008.

[19] See Soner Cagaptay, "Turkey's Local Elections: Liberal Middle Class Voters Abandon AKP," *PolicyWatch*, No. 1500, Washington Institute for Near East Policy, March 30, 2009. See also Soli Özel, "The Electorate's Tune-Up," *On Turkey*, German Marshall Fund of the United States, March 31, 2009.

The results of the March 2009 municipal elections were an important wake-up call. The AKP's popularity between 2002 and 2007 was based on the party's ability to put together a diverse coalition made up of big business, religious conservatives, ethnic minorities, and liberal democrats. The municipal elections indicate that this coalition has begun to erode, with large parts of the liberal middle class and Kurdish population defecting to other parties. The vote was seen as a referendum on the AKP's performance since the July 2007 election and as a warning sign that the party needs to rethink key aspects of its electoral strategy and policy agenda.

The AKP's political future will heavily depend on whether the party shows a renewed commitment to domestic reform and democratization or instead pursues a narrower, more religiously oriented agenda. If it moves in the latter direction, its popularity is likely to further decline, and Turkish politics could become increasingly fragmented and polarized.

Turkish democracy has been hindered by the lack of a strong secular opposition party. In recent years, the CHP, the main secular opposition party, has pursued an increasingly nationalistic and anti-Western policy. Instead of spearheading Turkey's EU-membership bid, the CHP has been one of the strongest critics of the EU and has given the impression that the party is little more than a stalking horse for the Turkish military.

The CHP's resistance to change has sharply reduced the party's popularity. The party has failed to poll more than 22–23 percent of the vote in recent elections and is badly in need of political rejuvenation and leadership change at the top. Deniz Baykal has been party leader for 20 years. During that period, the CHP has never won an election. However, Baykal faces no serious challenge to his leadership due to Turkey's archaic internal party structure, in which party leaders choose the party delegates, who are then beholden to the party leader for their positions and feel obligated to vote the leader back into power. This has allowed Baykal to retain tight control over the party and inhibited attempts to modernize the party and increase its capacity to address Turkey's growing political and social challenges.

Tensions with the Military

The recent internal polarization has been accentuated by tensions between the AKP and the military. Historically, the military has been a driving force behind Turkey's modernization. It sees itself as the guardian of Turkey's constitutional order, particularly secularism. On four occasions since the end of World War II, the military has intervened and ousted democratically elected civilian governments when it felt that there was a threat to Turkey's constitutional order. Each time, however, it has returned to the barracks after making what it considered to be necessary "corrections."

The 1982 constitution, hammered out by the military after the coup in 1980, upgraded the role of the Turkish National Security Council (NSC), which was dominated by the military, from an advisory body to one whose deliberations had to be given "priority" by the Council of Ministers. Although the NSC's statements were technically only recommendations, in practice, they were regarded as instructions to the civilian leadership. Failure to implement them could have serious consequences, as Prime Minister Necmettin Erbakan learned when he was ousted from office in a "soft coup" after he ignored the military's "advice" to take specific steps to curb anti-Islamic trends outlined in a NSC memorandum in February 1997.[20]

In recent years, however, the military's political influenced has diminished as a result of a number of important legislative changes designed to strengthen civilian control of the military and bring Turkish practices in line with those of the EU. Under the reform package introduced by the AKP in July 2003, the NSC was reduced to a truly advisory body, the requirement that the NSC secretary be a military officer was abolished, and the number of civilian members of the NSC was increased. Meetings were also reduced from once a month to once every two months. These changes made it more difficult for the military to use the NSC as a vehicle for exerting pressure on the civilian government.

_____

[20] For a detailed discussion of the military's role in Erbakan's ouster, see Rabasa and Larrabee, 2008, pp. 44–47.

The military leadership regards Islamic fundamentalism as a serious threat to Turkey's security and harbors deep-seated suspicions of the AKP because of the party's Islamic roots. Many officers believe that the AKP has a hidden agenda and fear that once the party has consolidated power, it will take steps designed to intensify the Islamization of Turkish social and political life. This has resulted in the emergence of an uneasy, at times adversarial, relationship marked by mistrust and suspicion on both sides.

Relations between the AKP and the military have fluctuated during the last decade. They were relatively smooth during General Hilmi Özkök's tenure as chief of the TGS (2002–2006). Özkök generally maintained a low profile and sought to work out a modus vivendi with the AKP. However, tensions increased under Özkök's successor, General Yasar Büyükanıt, former commander of the Land Forces. Büyükanıt was a strong secularist and took a tough line on the threat posed by Islamic fundamentalism and Kurdish separatism. He also publicly pressed for tougher military action against the PKK.

The nomination of Gül as the AKP's candidate for president brought tensions between the AKP and the military to a head in the spring of 2007. The decision prompted the TGS to issue a stern reminder on its Web site that the military took its responsibility to protect the constitution seriously and would act, when necessary, to carry out that responsibility. However, as noted earlier, the TGS's veiled threat of a possible coup if Gül were elected president backfired. Rather than discrediting the AKP, as was the TGS's intention, the memorandum served to increase support for the AKP in the July 2007 parliamentary elections.

The AKP's strong showing in the July 2007 elections was a direct slap in the face for the military and appears to have had a sobering impact on the TGS, which traditionally had been able to count on strong public support for its actions. Since the 2007 election, the military has been more circumspect in openly expressing its criticism. At the same time, in the aftermath of the ruling by the Constitutional Court regarding the closure of the AKP, Erdoğan has been careful to avoid taking steps that could antagonize the military.

Leadership changes in the top echelons of the military have also contributed to reducing civil-military tensions. General Ilker Başbuğ, who replaced Büyükanıt as chief of the TGS in August 2008, has been more circumspect in airing his views publicly than was Büyükanıt. He has also sought to open up lines of communication with the civilian sectors of society, particularly the media, and redefine the army's role in politics.[21] These moves have contributed to smoother civil-military relations.

In addition, the Turkish military's image and credibility were damaged by the PKK attacks at Aktunin in October 2008. The attacks came as a shock to the Turkish public because the military had been arguing that the PKK had been badly weakened and was on the defensive. But the Aktunin attack, which led to the death of 17 Turkish soldiers—the highest total since June 2004, when the PKK broke the ceasefire—demonstrated that the PKK was very much alive, and it generated strong criticism of the military in the Turkish press.[22]

The military's reputation has been particularly damaged by the arrest of several retired high-ranking military officers for alleged involvement in a plot to destabilize the AKP government—the so-called Ergenekon affair.[23] The officers appear to have been plotting a

---

[21] See his speech to the War Academies Command in Istanbul on April 24, 2009, in which he stressed the need to recognize subnational cultural identities, such as the Kurds, reiterated his support for a secular and democratic regime in Turkey, and called for a healthier civil military relationship. His speech represented a marked shift in the military's position on a number of social and political issues, especially religion. See Saban Kurdas, "Chief of the Turkish Army Redefining the Political Role of the Military," *Eurasia Daily Monitor*, Vol. 6, No. 72, April 15, 2009b.

[22] The public outcry was reinforced by a report in the Turkish daily *Taraf*, which has a reputation for hard-hitting investigative reporting, that the military had advance intelligence of the attack, and by the publication of a picture of the Turkish Air Force Commander General Aydoğan Babaoğlu playing golf at a resort on the day of the attack. See Yigal Schleifer, "Turkey's Army Loses Luster over PKK Attack," *Christian Science Monitor*, October 17, 2008. See also "Angeschlagenes Image der türkischen Armee," *Neue Zürcher Zeitung*, October 17, 2008.

[23] For background on the Ergenekon affair, see Ece Temelkuran, "Inside the Ergenekon Case," *CounterPunch*, December 4, 2008.

coup, which was blocked by Özkök when he was Chief of the TGS.[24] In addition, in June 2009, documents were leaked to the Turkish press suggesting that some officers in the TGS proposed a plan to discredit the AKP government and the Gülen movement.[25] These revelations have opened the military to an unprecedented degree of public criticism and scrutiny. Although the military still remains an influential force in Turkish politics, its image has been tarnished, and it is no longer considered untouchable, as was largely the case in the past.

In addition, the AKP has taken steps to further curb the independence and special status of the military. On June 26, 2009, the Turkish parliament passed a law that prohibits military courts from trying civilians and allows civilian courts to prosecute military officers. The law is intended to put an end to the abnormal status of the military courts and bring Turkish practices in line with those of the EU. However, the military has objected to the law, claiming it is unconstitutional.[26] If the law is upheld, it could lead to an escalation of tension between the military and the AKP leadership.

Over the longer term, the course of civil-military relations will heavily depend on the evolution of the Kurdish issue—especially the threat posed by the PKK—and on Erdoğan's willingness to refrain from taking measures that are perceived by the military as posing a threat to secularism. If the Kurdish issue heats up or Erdoğan faces growing pressure from within the AKP to pursue a more overtly Islamic agenda, tensions with the military could increase.

---

[24] In his testimony to the Ergenekon prosecutors, Özkök stated that he was informed about the coup plans but did not have sufficient evidence to do anything about them. See "Former Top General 'Knew Coup Plans,'" *Hürriyet Daily News and Economic Review* (Istanbul), July 22, 2009.

[25] On June 12, 2009, the Turkish daily *Taraf* published a leaked document, entitled "Plan to Combat Islamic Fundamentalism," which had allegedly originated in a department of the TGS. Although the authenticity of the document is unclear, its publication touched off a political firestorm and embarrassed the TGS. For details, see Amberlin Zaman, "Receding Power of the Military: A Leap for Democracy or Another Power Struggle?" *On Turkey*, German Marshall Fund of the United States, July 15, 2009c.

[26] "Soldiers Balk at Facing Civil Courts," *Hürriyet Daily News and Economic Review* (Istanbul), July 6, 2009.

A lot will also depend on Turkey's external security environment. The deterioration of Turkey's immediate security environment in recent years has served to strengthen the role of the military in Turkish politics. If Turkey's relations with its neighbors, particularly northern Iraq, become more stable and the threat posed by the PKK diminishes, the military is likely to be more willing to accept a reduction of its power and influence in Turkish politics. However, if the military sees growing external and internal threats to Turkey's security, it will be more inclined to resist measures that significantly circumscribe its autonomy and power.

The Impact of the Global Economic Crisis

The current global economic crisis could have an important impact on Turkey's political evolution and security ties, including those with the United States. As Lesser has noted, Turkey's economic and social development in recent years have been fueled by high growth rates—6–7 percent per annum since 2002—among the highest in the Organisation for Economic Co-operation and Development. High growth rates have been accompanied by large increases in foreign investment, and these increases have contributed to the growth of small- and medium-sized firms in Anatolia—the so-called Anatolian tigers—and provided an important stimulus for Turkey's economic and social transformation, fueling prosperity in Anatolia and changing the patterns of income distribution and influence in diverse sectors.[27] This growth has also contributed to an expanding real-estate market.

Until recently, many Turks had assumed that Turkey's economic development and prosperity could be decoupled from the global economic crisis. This, however, seems increasingly unlikely. Growth rates are projected to drop markedly in the next few years—perhaps to as low as 2–3 percent per year. Unemployment is also expected to rise as foreign investment slows. Turkey's construction industry has already

---

[27] Ian O. Lesser, "Turkey and the Global Economic Crisis," *On Turkey*, German Marshall Fund of the United States, December 1, 2008c.

witnessed a sharp contraction as credit has begun to dry up. Turkey has been negotiating a new standby loan with the International Monetary Fund, but any such loan is likely to involve strict conditionality and tight constraints on government spending.

The economic crisis is likely to have both domestic and foreign policy consequences. On the domestic side, one of the key victims could be the AKP. The AKP has presided over a period of high growth rates and economic expansion, which is one reason for its strong showing in the July 22, 2007, elections. Many Turkish voters were attracted by its laissez-faire economic policies, which seemed to promise greater economic prosperity. But with growth rates slowing, credit drying up, and the Turkish economy contracting, many Turks who supported the AKP in the past may begin to defect to other parties, especially those advocating populist and nationalist policies.

Defense budgets may also contract, slowing Turkey's military-modernization plans and creating new sources of tension with the military. And the AKP's expansive economic plans to develop Turkey's impoverished southeast may have to be shelved or curtailed, aggravating discontent among the predominantly Kurdish population of the region and fueling increased social tensions, which have lately shown signs of increasing.[28]

On the foreign-policy side, Turkey's relations with the EU, already damaged by the slowdown in the pace of domestic reform in Ankara, could be further strained by an economic recession in Europe, which could lead to tighter labor markets and increased restrictions on immigration and migrant labor, both of which would have a negative impact on Turkey. Trade with Russia—Turkey's second-largest trading partner—could also begin to slow. Turkish construction firms in

---

[28] In March 2008, Erdoğan announced a $12-billion economic plan to build two large dams and a system of water canals and to carry out road improvements in the southeast. These measures were designed to create jobs and reduce the attraction of the PKK. Much of the money, however, was allocated to projects already underway rather than to new investments. See Ümit Enginsoy and Burak Ede Bekdil, "Ankara Plans Economic, Other Improvements for Kurdish Areas," *Defense News*, March 17, 2008a.

Russia have already begun to feel the economic pinch as credit has become harder to obtain.[29]

Relations with the United States could also be affected. At a time of severe economic crisis, it may prove difficult for Ankara to get high-level attention from Washington. Key U.S. officials, preoccupied with mitigating the impact of the global economic crisis on the U.S. economy, may have less time to devote to Turkey—and to foreign policy more generally. There is thus a danger that important bilateral issues will get relegated to the backburner or simply not get the attention they deserve, increasing the chance that tensions may escalate and reach a crisis point while high-level U.S. attention is focused elsewhere.[30]

---

[29] Tuğba Tekerek, "Crisis Hits Turkish Projects in Russia," *Turkish Daily News* (Istanbul), October 18–19, 2008.

[30] The Armenian genocide issue is a perfect candidate in this category.

CHAPTER NINE

Alternative Turkish Futures

The future of the U.S.-Turkish partnership will depend heavily on Turkey's evolution in the coming decade. Depending on internal and external developments, Turkey could evolve in several different directions. This chapter examines several possible alternative futures and their implications for U.S. policy.

A Pro-Western Turkey Integrated into the European Union

In this scenario, Turkey would become a member of the EU or be well on its way to achieving membership within the coming decade. Although Turkey's economic level would remain below that of many EU members, the economic gap, spurred by continued high growth rates, would be narrowed. Turkey's human rights record would significantly improve, and civilian control of the military would be strengthened. The EU would abandon the goal of becoming a strong federal entity and become a looser confederation of nation-states, making Turkish membership in the EU easier to achieve and more politically acceptable to EU members.

Overall, this scenario would have positive benefits for the United States. It would enhance internal stability in Turkey and anchor Turkey in a broad Euro-Atlantic framework—one of the major goals of U.S. policy—thereby ending the debate about Turkey's long-term political orientation. It would also provide an important bridge to the Muslim world and could encourage the development of greater openness and political pluralism in the Muslim world more broadly. However, over the long run, it would also lead to a gradual weakening of Turkey's security ties to the United States. Increasingly, Ankara would look to Brussels, not Washington, in orienting its foreign policy. Over time, Turkey's policy would become more Europeanized, and Ankara would be even less willing to follow the U.S. lead on matters that affected Turkey's relations with Europe.

The likelihood that Turkey will become a member of the EU in the next decade, however, is slim. As noted in Chapter Six, popular opposition to Turkish membership in the EU is strong, particularly in France, Germany, and Austria. Many EU citizens simply do not regard Turkey as European on either political or cultural and religious grounds. The growth of Muslim communities in Europe over the last decade, together with growing concerns about terrorism more broadly, has reinforced European concerns about Turkish membership. The influence of the military in Turkish politics, though somewhat diminished in the last few years, remains an obstacle to Turkish EU membership, as does the lack of a Cyprus settlement. Finally, many Europeans are concerned that Turkey's problem with the Kurds and its proximity to the turbulent Middle East could result in these problems being imported into the EU if Turkey becomes a member.

Important signs that Turkey's chances of accession to the EU were improving would include continued momentum toward political reform in Turkey, particularly repeal of Article 301 of the Turkish penal code, which has been used to punish journalists and writers for insulting Turkishness; a more forthcoming attitude in Turkey toward minority rights, particularly the rights of the Kurds; stronger civilian control of the Turkish military; visible progress toward a Cyprus settlement; and movement within the EU toward a looser organization based on "variable geography" or "concentric circles."

If Turkey were to successfully complete accession negotiations on all 35 chapters, continue to improve its human rights record, continue to witness strong economic growth well above the EU average, and take visible steps to resolve its differences with the Kurds and promote a Cyprus settlement, a tipping point could be reached that would make it difficult—but not impossible—for the EU to reject Turkish membership.

An "Islamisized" Turkey

In this scenario, Turkey would increasingly stress its Muslim identity. Its ties to the West would weaken over the next decade, while those to the Islamic world would strengthen. Turkey would not go the way of Iran or adopt the shari'a as a fundamental principle of government, but its attachment to secularism and Western values would weaken. This could come about if (1) the Erdoğan leadership, which is composed of moderate Islamists, were replaced by a more radical Muslim leadership, (2) the EU continued to throw roadblocks in the way of Turkish membership, and (3) the United States failed to maintain sustained support for Turkey's campaign against the PKK. Under these circumstances, a bitter and frustrated Turkey might seek to strengthen ties to Muslim countries of the Middle East as an alterative to its strong ties to the West.

This scenario would have important negative implications for U.S.-Turkish relations. Turkey's ties to the West—and specifically to the United States—would significantly weaken. The U.S. ability to use Turkish bases would be sharply reduced, probably terminated. On many issues—especially those related to the Arab-Israeli conflict—Turkey would openly adopt a pro-Arab position. Turkish defense and intelligence cooperation with Israel would be sharply curtailed, probably ended. Security cooperation with Iran and Syria would increase. Turkey would withdraw from NATO and abandon efforts to join the EU.

If such a scenario were to transpire, the United States would have to reduce its defense footprint in Turkey and seek alternative access and base rights to carry out many of the missions currently being performed out of İncirlik Air Base. Loss of İncirlik would seriously impede the U.S. ability to conduct missions in Iraq. Today, nearly 70 percent of U.S. troops and materiel destined for Iraq transits through Turkey.

The chances of such a scenario materializing, however, are low—provided that the United States shows sensitivity to Turkey's most pressing security concerns, particularly its problems with the PKK. Turkey's commitment to secularism is strong. This is particularly true of the Turkish military, as its toughly worded memorandum in late April 2007 underscored. If the Turkish government showed serious signs of abandoning secularism, the military would almost certainly intervene. However, such a scenario could unfold if the United States fails to support Turkey's battle against the PKK forcefully and if the EU continues to raise new obstacles to Turkish membership.

Signs that Turkey was moving in a more-Islamist direction would include a weakening of secular control of education and the judiciary; a weakening of the military's influence in Turkish politics; increased domestic polarization between secularists and Islamists; growing pressure to prohibit the sale and consumption of alcohol; an intensification of Turkey's ties to Iran and other radical Muslim regimes; a significant strengthening of Turkish support for the Palestinian cause; an intensification of Turkey's ties to radical groups, such as Hezbollah and Hamas; and a decision by Turkey to withdraw from NATO.

The Islamization of Turkish foreign policy could be strengthen if Turkish relations with the United States and the EU continue to deteriorate and if the current moderate leadership in the AKP were replaced by a more radical Islamist leadership group.

A Nationalist Turkey

In this scenario, Turkey would move in a more nationalist direction. Frustrated by the EU's continuing obfuscation and tendency to impose new obstacles to its membership, Turkey would abandon its quest for EU membership but still maintain strong economic and trade ties to Europe. It would accept some form of privileged partnership with the EU along the lines currently proposed by the Christian Democratic Union in Germany and by Sarkozy in France. It would maintain important defense ties to the United States but pursue a more independent policy, especially toward the Middle East and Central Asia. Ties to Russia would be strengthened, particularly in the economic area. Defense cooperation with Moscow would be expanded. Turkey would also adopt a tougher position toward the Iraqi Kurds and be more willing to take unilateral military action against the PKK.

This scenario would make Turkey a more difficult partner for the United States. Although strong Turkish defense ties to the United States would continue to exist in certain specific areas, U.S. use of Turkish bases would be more constrained. Politically and militarily, the United States would not be able to rely on Turkish support, particularly on issues related to the Middle East. Turkey would also seek to further diversify its defense procurement sources.

This scenario is the most likely scenario over the medium term—especially if Turkey's relations with the United States and the EU continue to deteriorate. Signs that Turkey is moving in a more nationalistic direction would include a visible increase in popular support for nationalist political parties; an intensification of anti-Western rhetoric in the Turkish press; a failure to repeal Article 301 of the Turkish penal code; a more overtly hostile attitude toward minorities, particularly the Kurds; a resurgence of nationalist rhetoric over Cyprus; a weakening of rapprochement with Greece; growing antipathy toward the EU; and a weakening of ties to the United States and NATO.

Military Intervention

A fourth possibility is an escalation of political and social tensions in Turkey that leads to intervention by the Turkish military. A confrontation could take place if the AKP takes actions seen by the military as crossing important redlines. There are two possible variants of the intervention scenario: one is a "soft coup," in which the military would mobilize social pressure against an AKP-led government, eventually forcing it to resign. The other is a direct military intervention leading to the forcible removal of the AKP government and the disbandment of the party.

Although a direct intervention by the military cannot be excluded, especially if the AKP begins to push an Islamic agenda more aggressively, it is not very likely. The military would take this path only as a last resort after it had exhausted all other options. The military has been sobered by its previous direct interventions and has little enthusiasm for governing directly. In recent years, it has preferred to rely on indirect methods to achieve its goals.

Moreover, mobilizing society against the government, as the military did to force Prime Minister Erbakan's ouster in 1997, would be much harder to do against the AKP. The AKP was elected in a landslide victory with 47 percent of the vote. Unlike Erbakan's Welfare Party, which obtained only 21 percent of the vote, the AKP has broad-based popular support, having obtained the support of nearly half the voting electorate. Thus, unlike 1997, the military could not count on strong popular support for its action.

The strong public reaction to the military's midnight memorandum of April 27, 2007, with its veiled threat of military intervention, underscores this point. The AKP's landslide victory in the July 22, 2007, election represented a direct slap in the face for the military. Rather than rallying the population against the AKP, as it was intended to do, the memorandum actually increased support for the AKP. This fact is unlikely to be lost on the military and may make it cautious about openly trying to mobilize opposition to the AKP.

Direct military intervention—i.e., a military coup—would create difficulties for the United States. It would have a negative impact on Turkey's bid for EU membership and provoke a crisis in Turkey's relations with the EU. It would also contradict U.S. efforts to promote democratic reform in Turkey, accentuating tensions in U.S.-Turkish relations. Congress might impose sanctions or hold up the delivery of arms to Turkey. Passage of the Armenian Genocide Resolution would become more likely.

Moreover, there is no guarantee that the military would pursue a pro-Western course. Indeed, a military regime would probably pursue a more nationalistic course—a more acute version of the policy outlined in the nationalist scenario. Internally, the "deep state" (e.g., the powerful national-security bureaucracies that influence Turkish policy in nontransparent ways) would be strengthened. The military would take a harder line toward the Kurdish issue and overturn or reverse many of the liberal reforms introduced by the AKP (e.g., the introduction of Kurdish broadcasting and the use of the Kurdish language in schools), while in foreign policy, a military-led regime would likely pursue a tougher, more interventionist policy toward the KRG. It also would pursue a less active policy in the Middle East and be more inclined to adopt a tougher line on Cyprus. None of these positions would be welcome in Washington. In short, all in all, Turkey would become a much less attractive ally.

CHAPTER TEN

Conclusion: Revitalizing the U.S.-Turkish Relationship

A strong security partnership with Turkey has been an important element of U.S. policy in the Mediterranean and the Middle East for the last five decades. It is even more important today. Turkey plays a critical role in four areas of increasing strategic importance to the United States: the Middle East, the Persian Gulf, the Caucasus and Central Asia, and Europe. Thus, revitalizing the security partnership with Turkey and giving it new impetus should be a top U.S. policy priority.

Obama's trip to Turkey in April 2009 was an important first step in this process. During his visit, Obama succeeded in setting a new tone in bilateral relations and displayed a strong appreciation of the complexity of the domestic and foreign policy challenges that Turkey faces. However, one presidential visit, no matter how successful, cannot make up for years of neglect and mistrust. If the effort to revitalize U.S.-Turkish relations is to succeed, the visit needs to be followed up by concrete actions in a number of areas, outlined below.

Northern Iraq and the PKK

The United States should intensify its political and intelligence support for Turkey's struggle against PKK terrorism. U.S. support for Turkey's struggle against the PKK is regarded by Turkish officials as the litmus test of the value of the U.S.-Turkish security partnership.

The visible increase in anti-American sentiment in Turkey in recent years has been driven to an important degree by a perception that the United States is tacitly supporting the Iraqi Kurds. Strong support for Turkey's struggle against the PKK would have an important political-psychological impact on Turkish public opinion and help undermine this widespread perception.

In addition, the United States should put greater pressure on the KRG to crack down on the PKK and cease its logistical and political support of the group. Such pressure would have a positive impact on Washington's relations with Ankara and weaken the growth of anti-American sentiment among the general public in Turkey. However, anti-American sentiment in Turkey has complex roots and reflects more than just discontent with Bush's policy toward Iraq and the PKK. Thus, any shift in U.S. policy is likely to take longer to have a positive impact on public attitudes in Turkey than elsewhere in Europe.

The PKK threat cannot be resolved by military means. A strong antiterrorist program is essential, but to be successful, it must be combined with social and economic reforms that address the root causes of the Kurdish grievances. The Erdoğan government's "Kurdish Opening," launched in the summer of 2009, represents an encouraging sign that the government is beginning to recognize this. The initiative has sparked an intense internal debate in Turkey. If it proves successful, it could significantly reduce tensions between the Turkish authorities and the Kurdish community in Turkey and contribute to the wider process of democratization in the country.

The United States should strongly support Turkey's efforts to open a direct dialogue with the leadership of the KRG in northern Iraq. There can be no stability on Turkey's southern border over the long term without a Turkish accommodation with the KRG. This does not mean that Turkey should recognize an independent Kurdish state, but for regional stability to exist, Turkey needs to work out a modus vivendi with the KRG. Ultimately, this can only be achieved through a direct dialogue with the KRG leadership. The Erdoğan government has taken important steps in this direction since late 2008. Turkey and the KRG appear to be moving by fits and starts toward and important rapprochement. However, this rapprochement is fragile and needs strong U.S. support.

As the United States withdraws its forces from Iraq, it needs to intensify efforts to defuse tension between the KRG and the central government in Baghdad. This growing tension represents a serious threat to Iraq's viability as an integral state and could seriously complicate Turkey's security challenges. The U.S. military presence has acted as an important stabilizing force in northern Iraq and has helped prevent tension between the Iraqi Kurds and Arabs from breaking out into open conflict. But U.S. leverage and ability to influence the situation on the ground in Iraq will decline as the United States draws down its military forces. Thus, the United States needs to intensify efforts to get the two sides to resolve their political differences—especially their boundary disputes—*now* while Washington still has some political leverage. The United States should also maintain some military presence in northern Iraq as long as possible without violating the terms of the Status of Forces Agreement signed with the Maliki government at the end of 2008. This could help prevent current tension from escalating into open conflict as the two sides seek to resolve their political differences.

The Middle East

U.S. policymakers should avoid portraying Turkey as a model for the Middle East. The notion of Turkey as a model makes many Turks, especially the secularists and the military, uncomfortable because they feel it pushes Turkey politically closer to the Middle East and weakens Turkey's Western identity. In addition, they fear that it will strengthen political Islam in Turkey and erode the principle of secularism over the long run. These latter concerns are particularly strong within the Turkish armed forces.

The United States should continue to express a readiness to open a dialogue with Iran and Syria and to engage both countries in diplomatic efforts to help stabilize Iraq as it draws down its forces there. Such a move is unlikely to lead to dramatic changes in

Iranian or Syrian policy overnight. But it would make it harder for the regimes to blame the United States for the poor state of bilateral relations and could have important results over the long run. At the same time, it would bring U.S. and Turkish policy into closer alignment and reduce an important source of friction in U.S.-Turkish relations.

Washington should intensify its efforts to persuade Tehran to abandon any attempt to acquire nuclear weapons. A nuclear-armed Iran would have a destabilizing impact on security in the Persian Gulf region and could spark a nuclear arms race in the Gulf and Middle East, a race that could have important consequences for Turkish security. To date, Turkey has shown little interest in developing its own nuclear deterrent, and it is unlikely to do so as long as the U.S. nuclear guarantee and NATO remain credible. However, if Turkish relations with Washington and NATO deteriorate, Ankara might be prompted to consider acquiring a nuclear deterrent of its own. This underscores the importance of maintaining close U.S.-Turkish security ties and keeping Turkey firmly anchored in NATO.

Eurasia and the Caucasus

The United States should encourage and support Turkey's recent efforts to promote an improvement in relations with Armenia, particularly the opening of the border between the two. The normalization of relations between these two countries would significantly contribute to enhancing peace and stability in the Caucasus. It would also enable Armenia to reduce its economic and political dependence on Russia and Iran. Thus, a normalization of relations between Turkey and Armenia is strongly in U.S. interests.

In addition, the Obama administration should work closely with Congress to prevent the passage of an Armenian genocide resolution. The genocide issue is an emotionally charged issue in Turkey, especially among Turkish nationalists. Passage of such a resolution could cause the Turkish government to come under strong domestic pressure to take retaliatory action against the United States, possibly curtailing U.S. use of İncirlik Air Base. Such a move would have a significant impact on the ability of the United States to resupply its forces in Afghanistan, and it could complicate the withdrawal of U.S. combat forces from Iraq. At the same time, Turkey should be encouraged to address more openly the events surrounding the deaths of hundreds of Armenians at the hands of the Ottoman authorities in the final days of the Ottoman Empire. Clarification of the events during this tragic period is a prerequisite for a durable and lasting reconciliation with Armenia and would enhance Turkey's reputation as an open and modern democratic state.

Turkish Membership in the European Union

The United States should continue to support Turkey's membership in the EU. Turkey's integration into the EU would strengthen the EU and help put to rest the claim that the West—especially Europe—is innately hostile to Muslims. This could have a salutary effect on the West's relations with the Muslim world. Indeed, a moderate, democratic Turkey could act as an important bridge to the Middle East. On the other hand, rejection of Turkey's candidacy could provoke an anti-Western backlash, strengthening those forces in Turkey that want to weaken Turkey's ties to the West. Such a development is in the interest of neither the EU nor the United States.

However, given the sensitivity of the issue of Turkey's EU membership among EU member states, the United States should quietly support Turkish membership behind the scenes and avoid overt pressure and arm-twisting. As Sarkozy's strong rebuke of Obama's support for Turkish EU membership during the latter's visit to Ankara underscores, such tactics could provoke resentment among EU members and even hurt Turkey's chance for membership.

At the same time, Washington needs to recognize that Turkish membership in the EU—if it occurs—would alter the tone and character of U.S.-Turkish relations over the long run. Although Ankara will continue to want strong security ties to Washington, Turkish leaders would look increasingly to Brussels rather than Washington on many issues. As a result, Turkey's foreign policy would likely become more Europeanized over time.

Turkish-Greek Relations and Cyprus

The United States should intensify efforts to get Greece and Turkey to resolve their differences over the Aegean. Although Turkish-Greek relations have significantly improved since 1999, differences over the Aegean continue to mar bilateral relations and represent a threat to stability in the Eastern Mediterranean. Unless these differences are resolved, there is a danger that some incident could escalate out of control and lead to armed conflict, as almost happened over the islets of Imia/Kardak in February 1996. At a time when NATO faces serious challenges in Afghanistan and the post-Soviet space, the last thing the United States needs is a new crisis in the Aegean. Moreover, the incidents have a corrosive effect on the overall tenor of Turkish-Greek relations, making other bilateral issues harder to resolve.

The United States should also encourage and support the intensification of the intercommunal dialogue being conducted under UN auspices between the two Cypriot communities. Although the danger of Turkish-Greek conflict over Cyprus has receded in recent years, the lack of a Cyprus settlement remains an important obstacle to Turkey's aspirations for EU membership. Progress toward a settlement of the Cyprus dispute would give Turkey's membership bid critical new momentum at a time when accession negotiations have visibly slowed. It would also contribute to greater overall security and stability in the Eastern Mediterranean.

Defense Cooperation

In the wake of the Obama visit, Washington should initiate a broad strategic dialogue with Ankara about the future use of Turkish bases, particularly İncirlik. Given Turkey's growing interests and increasingly active policy in the Middle East, Ankara is likely to be highly sensitive about allowing the United States to use Turkish bases, especially İncirlik, for Middle East contingencies. The United States therefore cannot assume that it will have automatic use of Turkish bases in Middle East contingencies unless such use is regarded as being in Turkey's direct national interest.

The United States should review its rules and regulations regarding technology transfer to see whether some of the current restrictions could be eased without jeopardizing U.S. national security interests. These restrictions have been one of the main factors responsible for the sharp decline in commercial military sales to Turkey in recent years. Increasing Turkish frustration with these restrictions has prompted Turkey to turn to other weapon suppliers, such as Israel, South Korea, and Italy, that do not impose such strict restrictions on the sale of weapons and military equipment.

Ballistic missile defense could be an important area for future U.S.-Turkish defense cooperation. In light of the growing threat posed by the possible acquisition of nuclear weapons by Iran, the United States should explore missile-defense options, both bilaterally and through NATO, to ensure that Turkish territory is protected against the growing threat posed from ballistic missiles launched from the Middle East.

Democratization and Domestic Reform

The United States should encourage Turkey to revitalize the process of democratization and domestic reform. Although the Erdoğan government pursued a reformist agenda during its first several years, the process of democratization and domestic reform has visibly slowed since 2005 and needs new impetus. These reforms are necessary not only to give Turkey's EU membership bid new traction—they are also important in their own right.

The United States should not overreact to the growth of religious consciousness in Turkey. Turkish Islam is more moderate and pluralistic than Islam elsewhere in the Middle East. Turkey's long history of seeking to fuse Islam and Western influences dates back to the late Ottoman period. This history differentiates Turkey from other Muslim countries in the Middle East and enhances the chances that Turkey will be able to avoid the sharp dichotomies, ruptures, and violence that have characterized the process of political modernization in the Middle East.

These steps will not resolve all difficulties in U.S.-Turkish relations. Differences on some issues are bound to occur. However, taken together, these steps would go a long way toward revitalizing the U.S.-Turkish security partnership and make the remaining differences much easier to resolve.

Bibliography

Akyol, Mustafa, "Kurdish Nationalism on the Rise, Ballot Suggests," *Hürriyet Daily News and Economic Review* (Istanbul), May 31, 2009.

"Angela Merkel et Recep Tayyip Erdogan s'affrontent sur l'intégration des Turcs d'Allemagne," *Le Monde* (Paris), February 14, 2008.

"Angeschlagenes Image der türkischen Armee," *Neue Zürcher Zeitung*, October 17, 2008.

Aras, Bülent, "Turkey Between Syria and Israel: Turkey's Rising Soft Power," *SETA Policy Brief*, No. 15, May 2008.

———, "Davutoglu Era in Turkish Foreign Policy," *SETA Policy Brief*, No. 32, May 2009.

Aras, Bülent, and Fatih Özbay, "Turkish-Armenian Relations: Will Football Diplomacy Work?" *SETA Policy Brief*, No. 24, September 2008.

"Armenians and Turks Have Far to Go on Genocide," *International Herald Tribune*, September 1, 2009.

Arslan, Zühtü, "Turkey's Bid for the New Constitution," *Insight Turkey*, Vol. 9, No. 3, 2007.

Aslan, Azad, and Karim Wali, "Interview with David Phillips on 'Mapping Issues Between Turks and Iraqi Kurds,'" *Kurdish Globe*, May 31, 2009.

Aytürk, İlker, "Between Crises and Cooperation: The Future of Turkish-Israeli Relations," *Insight Turkey*, Vol. 11, No. 2, 2009.

Ayvaz, Tutku, "Turk Defense Industry Makes Strides," *Turkish Daily News* (Istanbul), December 27, 2007.

Bacık, Gökhan, "Turkish-Israeli Relations after Davos: A View from Turkey," *Insight Turkey*, Vol. 11, No. 2, 2009.

"Banning Kurdish Was a Mistake," *Turkish Daily News* (Istanbul), November 16, 2007.

Baran, Zeyno, "Turkey: Partnership on the Brink," *Journal of International Security Affairs*, No. 15, Fall 2008.

Barkey, Henri J., "The Struggles of a 'Strong' State," *Journal of International Affairs*, Vol. 54, No. 2, Fall 2000.

———, "Kurdistandoff," *The National Interest*, July/August 2007a.

———, "Notes from a Funeral," *The American Interest*, July/August 2007b.

———, *Preventing Conflict over Kurdistan*, Carnegie Endowment for International Peace, 2009.

Barkey, Henri J., and Graham E. Fuller, *Turkey's Kurdish Question*, Lanham, Md.: Rowman & Littlefield Publishers, 1998.

Barysch, Katinka, Steven Everts, and Heather Grabbe, *Why Europe Should Embrace Turkey*, London: Centre for European Reform, 2005.

Bekdil, Burak, "An Incursion Which Is Not—and Russsophiles in Ankara," *Turkish Daily News* (Istanbul), June 8, 2007.

Birand, Mehmet Ali, "Bush Didn't Risk Losing Turkey," *Turkish Daily News* (Istanbul), November 7, 2007.

Blank, Stephen, "Azerbaijan: Russia Is Increasingly Nervous About Its Grip on Caspian Energy," *Eurasia Insight*, Eurasianet.org, March 30, 2009.

Boro, İsmail, *Die getürke Republik: Woran die Integration in Deutschland scheitert*, Munich: Verlagsgruppe Random House, 2008.

Bozkurt, Göksel, "Kurdish Hopes in Turkish State," *Turkish Daily News* (Istanbul), November 12, 2007.

Cagaptay, Soner, "Turkey at a Crossroads: Preserving Ankara's Western Orientation," *Policy Focus*, No. 48, Washington Institute for Near East Policy, October 2005.

———, "Secularism and Foreign Policy in Turkey: New Elections, Troubling Trends," *Policy Focus*, No. 67, Washington Institute for Near East Policy, April 2007.

———, "Turkey's Local Elections: Liberal Middle Class Voters Abandon AKP," *PolicyWatch*, No. 1500, Washington Institute for Near East Policy, March 30, 2009.

Çandar, Cengiz, "Turkey Needs to Approach Arbil for Oil Exportation," *Turkish Daily News* (Istanbul), March 19, 2007a.

———, "The Results from the White House; PKK's Elimination Process," *Turkish Daily News* (Istanbul), November 9, 2007b.

Çarkoğlu, Ali, "Turkey's Local Elections of 2009: Winners and Losers," *Insight Turkey*, Vol. 11, No. 2, 2009.

Çarkoğlu, Ali, and Binnaz Toprak, *Degisen Turkiye . . . 'de Din Toplum ve Slyaset*, Istanbul: Turkish Economic and Social Studies Foundation, 2006.

Cloud, David, "U.S. Seeks Alternatives If Turkey Cuts Off Access," *New York Times*, October 11, 2007.

"Conservative But Relaxed About It," *Turkish Daily News* (Istanbul), September 20–21, 2008.

Cornell, Svante E., and Halil Magnus Karaveli, "Prospects for a 'Torn' Turkey: A Secular and Unitary Future?" Silk Road Paper, Central Asia-Caucasus Institute & Silk Road Studies Program, October 2008.

Dagher, Sam, "Kurds Lay Claim to Land and Oil, Defying Baghdad," *New York Times*, July 10, 2009.

Dağı, İhsan, "AK Party Survives Closure Case: What Is Next?" *SETA Policy Brief*, No. 19, August 2008.

Daly, John, *U.S.-Turkish Relations: A Strategic Relationship Under Stress*, Washington, D.C.: Jamestown Foundation, February 2008.

Demirel, Tanel, "Civil-Military Relations in Turkey: Two Patterns of Civilian Behavior Towards the Military," *Turkish Studies*, Vol. 4, No. 3, Autumn 2003.

Demirtas, Serkan, "Blackseafor to Be Expanded," *Turkish Daily News* (Istanbul), September 19, 2008.

———, "New Political Guidance Needed for Turkey-Greece Ties," *Hürriyet Daily News and Economic Review* (Istanbul), May 18, 2009.

"Die Türkei-Frage spaltet Armenien," *Neue Zürcher Zeitung*, May 13, 2009.

Enginsoy, Ümit, "US Intel Aid Implied in Strike on PKK," *Turkish Daily News* (Istanbul), December 3, 2007.

———, "No Change Wanted on Turk Straits Convention," *Turkish Daily News* (Istanbul), August 28, 2008.

Enginsoy, Ümit, and Burak Ege Bekdil, "Turkey Will Not Back U.S. Military Action on Iran," *Defense News*, December 6, 2004.

———, "Turks Oppose US Black Sea Move," *Defense News*, March 13, 2006.

———, "Turkey Modernizes to Face Mid East Threats," *Defense News*, April 23, 2007a.

———, "Turkey Increasingly Shuns US Weapons," *Defense News*, July 7, 2007b.

———, "Turkish-Iranian Rapprochement Worries US," *Defense News*, August 6, 2007c.

———, "Amid Squabbles, Turkish Military, Civilians Agree to Buy Locally," *Defense News*, September 10, 2007d.

———, "US Backs Turkey's Anti-PKK Strikes," *Defense News*, December 10, 2007e.

———, "Ankara Plans Economic, Other Improvements for Kurdish Areas," *Defense News*, March 17, 2008a.

———, "Turkey Jealously Defends Its Rights on the Black Sea," *Defense News*, September 29, 2008b.

———, "Turkey Agrees to Help U.S. Withdrawal from Iraq," *Defense News*, March 30, 2009a.

———, "U.S., Turkey Work on Super Cobra Sale," *Defense News*, June 15, 2009b.

"Erdogan in Kreuzfeuer der Kritik," *Neue Zürcher Zeitung*, November 2, 2008.

"Erdogan's Kölner Rede," *Frankfurter Allgemeine Zeitung*, February 15, 2008.

Ergin, Sedat, "The Perfect Crisis Revisited: The Story of the March 1, 2003 Motion," *Private View*, No. 13, Autumn 2008.

European Security Initiative, *Sex and Power in Turkey: Feminism, Islam and the Maturing of Turkish Democracy*, Berlin, June 2, 2007.

Fata, Dan, "Testimony for Mr. Daniel Fata, Deputy Assistant Secretary for Europe and NATO, U.S. House of Representatives House Committee on Foreign Affairs," *Insight Turkey*, Vol. 9, No. 1, 2007.

"Fewer Israeli Tourists After Davos Outburst," *Hürriyet Daily News and Economic Review* (Istanbul), June 14, 2009.

Flanagan, Stephen J., and Samuel J. Brannen, *Turkey's Evolving Dynamics: Strategic Choices for U.S.-Turkey Relations*, Washington, D.C.: Center for Strategic & International Studies, 2009.

"Former Top General 'Knew Coup Plans,'" *Hürriyet Daily News and Economic Review* (Istanbul), July 22, 2009.

Gardner, David, "Iran's Divided Regime Prevails—at the Cost of Its Legitimacy," *Financial Times* (London), August 8, 2009.

Gordon, Philip, and Ömer Taşpınar, "Turkey on the Brink," *Washington Quarterly*, Vol. 29, No. 3, Summer 2006.

———, *Winning Turkey: How America, Europe, and Turkey Can Revive a Fading Partnership*, Washington, D.C.: Brookings Institution Press, 2008.

Görener, Aylin S., "Turkey and Northern Iraq on the Course of Raprochement [sic]," *SETA Policy Brief*, No. 17, June 2008.

Görgülü, Aybars, "Towards a Turkish-American Rapprochement?" *Insight Turkey*, Vol. 11, No. 2, 2009.

"Greek FM Concerned About Rising Tension," *Hurriyet Daily News and Economic Review* (Istanbul), June 24, 2009.

Gül, Abdullah, "Turkey's Role in a Changing Middle East Environment," *Mediterranean Quarterly*, Vol. 15, No. 1, Winter 2004.

Gülmez, Seçkin Barış, "The EU Policy of the Republican People's Party: An Inquiry on the Opposite Party and Euro-Skepticism in Turkey," *Turkish Studies*, Vol. 9, No. 3, September 2008.

Hale, William, *Turkey, the U.S. and Iraq*, London: SOAS, London Middle East Institute, 2007.

Harris, George S., *Troubled Alliance: Turkish-American Problems in Historical Perspective, 1945–1971*, Washington, D.C.: American Enterprise Institute for Public Policy Research, 1972.

Harris Interactive, "Financial Times/Harris Poll: EU Citizens Want Referendum on Treaty," Web page, June 18, 2007. As of June 22, 2009:
http://www.harrisinteractive.com/news/allnewsbydate.asp?NewsID=1228

Heper, Metin, "The Problem of the Strong State for the Consolidation of Democracy," *Comparative Political Studies*, Vol. 25, July 1992.

Hermann, Rainer, *Wohin geht die türkische Gesellschaft? Kulturkampf in der Türkei*, Munich: Deutscher Taschenbuch Verlag GmbH&Co, 2008.

Hug, Adam, ed., *Turkey in Europe: The Economic Case for Turkish Membership of the EU*, London: Foreign Policy Centre, 2008. As of January 27, 2009:
http://fpc.org.uk/fsblob/991.pdf

İdiz, Semih, "PKK Assures Unsavory Developments for All," *Turkish Daily News* (Istanbul), June 15, 2007a.

———, "The Erdogan-Bush Talks: Successful or Not?" *Turkish Daily News* (Istanbul), November 9, 2007b.

———, "A New Era in Turkish Kurdish Ties," *Hürriyet Daily News and Economic Review* (Istanbul), March 20, 2009.

International Crisis Group, "Islam and Identity in Germany," Europe Report No. 181, Washington, D.C.: International Crisis Group, March 14, 2007a.

———, "Iraq and the Kurds: Resolving the Kirkuk Crisis," Middle East Report No. 64, Washington, D.C.: International Crisis Group, April 19, 2007b.

———, "Oil for Soil: Toward a Grand Bargain on Iraq and the Kurds," Middle East Report No. 80, Washington, D.C.: International Crisis Group, October 2008a.

———, "Turkey and Iraqi Kurds: Conflict or Cooperation," Middle East Report No. 81, Washington, D.C.: International Crisis Group, November 13, 2008b.

———, "Iraq and the Kurds: Trouble Along the Trigger Line," Middle East Report No. 88, Washington, D.C.: July 8, 2009a.

————, "Kurdish Opening Opens Minds," *Hürriyet Daily News and Economic Review* (Istanbul), August 14, 2009b.

"Iran Opposes Turkish Incursion into Iraq," *Turkish Daily News* (Istanbul), July 17, 2007.

"Israel zeigt der Türkei die kalte Schulter," *Neue Zürcher Zeitung*, August 14, 2009.

"Israeli Operation Draws Ire in Turkey," *The Probe* (Istanbul), May 23, 2004.

Janabi, Nazar, "Iranian Threats and UN Sanctions Debate," *PolicyWatch*, No. 1335, Washington Institute for Near East Policy, January 30, 2008.

Jenkins, Gareth, "Context and Circumstance: The Turkish Military and Politics," Adelphi Paper No. 337, International Institute for Strategic Studies, 2001.

————, "Continuity and Change: Prospects for Civil-Military Relations in Turkey," *International Affairs*, Vol. 83, No. 2, 2007a.

————, "Turkey Trying to Go Local in Defense Procurement," *Eurasia Daily Monitor*, Vol. 4, No. 226, December 6, 2007b.

————, "Turkey and Northern Iraq: An Overview," Occasional Paper, Jamestown Foundation, February 2008a.

————, "Turkey Bites the Bullet," *Eurasia Daily Monitor*, Vol. 5, No. 196, October 14, 2008b.

Kalın, İbrahim, "Turkey and the Middle East: Ideology or Geo-Politics?" *Private View*, No. 13, Autumn 2008.

Kapsis, James E., "From Desert Storm to Metal Storm: How Iraq Has Spoiled U.S.-Turkish Relations," *Current History*, November 2005.

Karabelias, Gerassimos, "Dictating the Upper Tide: Civil-Military Relations in the Post-Ozal Decade, 1993–2003," *Turkish Studies*, Vol. 9, No. 3, September 2008.

Karakas, Cemal, *Turkey: Islam and Laicism Between the Interests of the State, Politics and Society*, Report No. 78, Peace Research Institute Frankfurt (PIRF), 2007.

Karakaya, Rabia, "The AKP and the Kurdish Issue: What Went Wrong?" *SETA Policy Brief*, No. 14, May 2008.

Karasar, Hasan Ali, "Saakashvili Pulled the Trigger: Turkey Between Russia and Georgia," *SETA Policy Brief*, No. 20, August 2008.

Kardaş, Şaban, "Turkey Confronts a Disputed Period in Its History," *Eurasia Daily Monitor*, Vol. 5, No. 240, December 17, 2008.

————, "Gul Denies Saying 'Kurdistan' During Iraq Visit," *Eurasia Daily Monitor*, Vol. 6, No. 60, March 30, 2009a.

————, "Chief of the Turkish Army Redefining the Political Role of the Military," *Eurasia Daily Monitor*, Vol. 6, No. 72, April 15, 2009b.

————, "Opposition Rejects Gul's Call for Consensus on the Kurdish Issue," *Eurasia Daily Monitor*, Vol. 6, No. 96, May 19, 2009c.

Katz, Yaavov, "Navy to Partake in Turkish Exercise," *Jerusalem Post*, August 11, 2009.

"Kein Assimilationsdruck," *Frankfurter Allgemeine Zeitung*, February 13, 2008.

Kılınç, General Tuncer, speech at the War Academy, Istanbul, March 7, 2002.

Kınıklıoğlu, Suat, "The Anatomy of Turkish-Russian Relations," *Insight Turkey*, Vol. 8, No. 2, April–June 2006.

Kinzer, Stephen, "Turkey Finds European Door Slow to Open," *New York Times*, February 23, 1997.

Kupchinsky, Roman, "Azerbaijan and Russia Ink Tentative Gas Agreement," *Eurasia Daily Monitor*, Vol. 6, No. 62, April 1, 2009.

Laçiner, Sedat, Mehmet Özcan, and İhsan Bal, *European Union with Turkey: The Possible Impact of Turkey's Membership on the European Union*, Ankara: International Strategic Research Organisation, 2005.

Larrabee, F. Stephen, "Turkey Rediscovers the Middle East," *Foreign Affairs*, Vol. 86, No. 4, July/August 2007.

Larrabee, F. Stephen, and Ian O. Lesser, *Turkish Foreign Policy in an Age of Uncertainty*, Santa Monica, Calif.: RAND Corporation, MR-1612-CMEPP, 2003. As of June 22, 2009:
http://www.rand.org/pubs/monograph_reports/MR1612/

Laruelle, Marlène, "Russo-Turkish Rapprochement Through the Idea of Eurasia: Alexander Dugin's Networks in Turkey," Occasional Paper, Jamestown Foundation, April 30, 2008.

Lesser, Ian O., "Turkey, the United States, and the Geopolitics of Delusion," *Survival*, Vol. 48, No. 3, Autumn 2006.

————, *Beyond Suspicion: Rethinking US-Turkish Relations*, Washington, D.C.: Woodrow Wilson Center, 2007.

————, "After Georgia: Turkey's Looming Foreign Policy Dilemmas," *On Turkey*, German Marshall Fund of the United States, August 26, 2008a.

————, "Turkey and *Transatlantic Trends*: How Distinctive?" *On Turkey*, German Marshall Fund of the United States, September 15, 2008b.

————, "Turkey and the Global Economic Crisis," *On Turkey*, German Marshall Fund of the United States, December 1, 2008c.

————, "The Obama Visit and After: Changing Style and Substance in U.S.-Turkish Relations," *On Turkey*, German Marshall Fund of the United States, April 14, 2009a.

————, "Russia, Europe, Iran: Three Grand Strategic Issues in U.S.-Turkish Relations," *On Turkey*, German Marshall Fund of the United States, June 19, 2009b.

Luft, Stefan, "Assimilation, Integration, Identität," *Frankfurter Allgemeine Zeitung*, February 15, 2008.

Marcus, Aliza, *Blood and Belief: The PKK and the Kurdish Fight for Independence*, New York: New York University Press, 2007a.

————, "Turkey's PKK: Rise, Fall, and Rise Again?" *World Policy Journal*, Vol. 24, No. 1, Spring 2007b.

Mardin, Serif, "Center-Periphery Relations: A Key to Turkish Politics?" *Daedalus*, Vol. 102, No. 1, 1973.

————, "Turkish Islamic Exceptionalism, Yesterday and Today: Continuity, Rupture and Reconstruction in Operational Codes," *Journal of International Affairs*, Vol. 54, No. 1, Fall 2000.

"Merkel: Ich bin auch Kanzlerin der Turken in Deutschland," *Frankfurter Allgemeine Zeitung*, February 12, 2008.

Mufson, Steven, "Kurdish Ministers Woo U.S. Oil Firms," *Washington Post*, November 28, 2007.

Murinson, Alexander, "Azerbaijan-Turkey-Israel Relations: The Energy Factor," *Middle East Review of International Affairs*, Vol. 12, No. 3, September 2008.

"Nabucco Project Not in EU Pipeline," *Hürriyet Daily News and Economic Review* (Istanbul), March 18, 2009.

Narlı, Nilüfer, "Civil-Military Relations in Turkey," *Turkish Studies*, Vol. 1, No. 1, Spring 2000.

Neumann, Iver B., *Uses of the Other: The "East" in European Identity Formation*, Minneapolis: University of Minnesota Press, 1999.

Öniş, Ziya, "Turkey-EU Relations: Beyond the Current Stalemate," *Insight Turkey*, Vol. 10, No. 4, 2008a.

Oppel, Richard A., Jr., "Kurds Reach New Oil Deals, Straining Ties with Baghdad," *New York Times*, October 4, 2007.

"Outlines of a Kurdish Deal loom in N. Iraq," *Hürriyet Daily News and Economic Review* (Istanbul), March 19, 2009.

Özel, Soli, "Will Turkey Opt Out?" *On Turkey*, German Marshall Fund of the United States, September 15, 2008a.

————, "The Battle of Giants," *On Turkey*, German Marshall Fund of the United States, September 30, 2008b.

————, "Committed to Change, or Changing Commitments? Turkish-American Relations Under a New U.S. President," *On Turkey*, German Marshall Fund of the United States, November 17, 2008c.

————, "The Electorate's Tune-Up," *On Turkey*, German Marshall Fund of the United States, March 31, 2009.

Özerkan, Fulya, "Israel Snubs Offer of Channel to Syria," *Hürriyet Daily News and Economic Review* (Istanbul), August 14, 2009.

"Ozkok Talks Tough," *Turkish Daily News* (Istanbul), April 21, 2005.

"Ozkok: Turkei kein Modell," *Frankfurter Allgemeine Zeitung*, April 22, 2005.

Parris, Mark R., "Memorandum to President-Elect Obama, re: Turkey," *Private View*, No. 13, Autumn 2008.

Pew Global Attitudes Project, *Global Unease with Major Powers*, Pew Research Center, June 27, 2007.

————, *Confidence in Obama Lifts U.S. Image Around the World: Most Muslim Publics Not So Easily Moved*, Pew Research Center, July 23, 2009.

"PKK Issue Should Have Been Resolved in Its Social Stage," *Turkish Daily News* (Istanbul), November 12, 2007.

"Prime Minister Objects to 'Moderate Islam' Label," *Hürriyet Daily News and Economic Review* (Istanbul), April 4–5, 2009.

"Public Opposition to Turkey's Entry Growing Stronger in the EU," *Today's Zaman* (Istanbul), June 19, 2007.

Rabasa, Angel, and F. Stephen Larrabee, *The Rise of Political Islam in Turkey*, Santa Monica, Calif.: RAND Corporation, MG-726-OSD, 2008. As of June 22, 2009: http://www.rand.org/pubs/monographs/MG726/

Randal, Jonathan C., *After Such Knowledge, What Forgiveness? My Encounters with Kurdistan*, Boulder, Colo.: Westview Press, 1999.

Recknagel, Charles, "Iraq, Turkey Nearing Deal to Deprive PKK of Bases," Radio Free Europe/Radio Liberty, March 24, 2009.

Ribin, Alissa J., and Andrew E. Kramer, "Official Calls Kurd Oil Deal at Odds with Baghdad," *New York Times*, September 28, 2007.

Salaheddin, Sinan, "Turkish Officials Meet Iraqi Kurds in Baghdad," *Boston Globe*, October 15, 2008.

Schleifer, Yigal, "Turkey's Army Loses Luster over PKK Attack," *Christian Science Monitor*, October 17, 2008.

————, "Turkey: Iran Upheaval Poses Diplomatic Challenge for Ankara," *Eurasianet*, June 25, 2009.

Sezgin, Yuksel, "The October 1998 Crisis in Turkish-Syrian Relations: A Prospect Theory Approach," *Turkish Studies*, Vol. 3, No. 2, Autumn 2002.

Shadid, Anthony, "Kurdish Leaders Warn of Strains with Maliki," *New York Times*, July 17, 2009.

Socor, Vladimir, "Chancellor Merkel Says Nein to Nabucco," *Eurasia Daily Monitor*, Vol. 6, No. 45, March 9, 2009a.

———, "The Strategic Implications of Russian Move Against Hungary's MOL," *Eurasia Daily Monitor*, Vol. 6, No. 77, April 22, 2009b.

"Soldiers Balk at Facing Civil Courts," *Hürriyet Daily News and Economic Review* (Istanbul), July 6, 2009

Strauss, Delphine, and Ed Cooks, "Iraq Offers Half Gas Needed for Nabucco," *Financial Times* (London), July 13, 2009

Taşpınar, Ömer, "Turkey's Middle East Policies: Between Neo-Ottomanism and Kemalism," Carnegie Paper No. 10, September 2008.

Tavernise, Sabrina, and Sebnem Arsu, "Gas Pipeline Through Turkey Gains Backing in Europe," *New York Times*, July 14, 2009.

Tekerek, Tuğba, "Crisis Hits Turkish Projects in Russia," *Turkish Daily News* (Istanbul), October 18–19, 2008.

Temelkuran, Ece, "Inside the Ergenekon Case," *CounterPunch*, December 4, 2008.

Tezel, Yahya Sezai, *Transformation of State and Society in Turkey: From the Ottoman Empire to the Turkish Republic*, Ankara: Roma Publications, 2005.

Toprak, Binnaz, "The State, Politics and Religion in Turkey," in Metin Heper and Ahmet Evin, eds., *State, Democracy and the Military: Turkey in the 1980s*, Berlin/New York: Walter de Gruyter, 1988, pp. 119–136.

Torbakov, Igor, *The Georgia Crisis and Russia-Turkey Relations*, Washington, D.C.: Jamestown Foundation, 2008.

Tosun, Tanju, "The July 22 Elections: A Chart for the Future of Turkish Politics," *Private View*, No. 12, Autumn 2007.

Transatlantic Trends, *Transatlantic Trends: Key Findings 2006*, Washington, D.C.: German Marshall Fund of the United States, 2006.

———, *Transatlantic Trends: Key Findings 2007*, Washington, D.C.: German Marshall Fund of the United States, 2007.

———, *Transatlantic Trends: Key Findings 2008*, Washington, D.C.: German Marshall Fund of the United States, 2008.

Tuncay, Ebru, "Turkey the Winner in Gulf's Investment Hunt," *Hürriyet Daily News and Economic Review* (Istanbul), September 1, 2008.

Turan, İlter, "War at Home, Peace Abroad!" *Private View*, No. 13, Autumn 2008.

Turgut, Pelin, "Exports: Trade with Middle East Soars as Relationships Thaw," *Financial Times* (London), November 28, 2008.

"Turkey Irked by Gaza Offensive But Not Prompted to Reverse Ties to Israel," *The Probe* (Istanbul), May 30, 2004.

"Turkey OK with UN Report," *Hürriyet Daily News and Economic Review* (Istanbul), May 8, 2009.

"Turkey Refuses to Back Down on Iranian Energy Deal," *Eurasia Daily Monitor*, Vol. 4, No. 157, August 13, 2007.

"Turkey to Buy Weapons from US," *Hurriyet Daily News and Economic Review* (Istanbul), June 24, 2009.

Turkish General Staff, press release, April 27, 2007.

Turkish Industrialists' and Businessmen's Association, *Rebuilding a Partnership: Turkish-American Relations for a New Era—A Turkish Perspective*, Istanbul: TÜSİAD, April 2009.

Tyson, Ann Scott, and Robin Wright, "U.S. Helps Turkey Hit Rebel Kurds in Iraq," *Washington Post*, December 18, 2007.

Ulusoy, Kivanç, "Turkey and the EU: Democratization, Civil-Military Relations and the Cyprus Issue," *Insight Turkey*, Vol. 10, No. 4, 2008.

"Unneighborliness in Neighborhoods," *Hürriyet Daily News and Economic Review* (Istanbul), June 5, 2009.

"US Considers Shifting New F-16s to Incirlik, Report Says," *Turkish Daily News* (Istanbul), June 5, 2004.

"US Critical of Turkey's Partnership with Iran," *Turkish Daily News* (Istanbul), April 7, 2007.

"US Criticizes Turkey for Iran Energy Deal," *Turkish Daily News* (Istanbul), September 22–23, 2007.

"US: No Letup in Efforts for Broader Use of Incirlik," *Turkish Daily News* (Istanbul), August 18, 2007.

"U.S. Rules Out Iranian Role for Nabucco," UPI.com, March 30, 2009.

"US Uneasy over Turkey Iran Gas Deal," *Turkish Daily News* (Istanbul), July 12, 2007.

Uslu, Emrullah, "Gul's Visit to Baghdad: A Sign of Rapprochement with the Kurds?" *Eurasia Daily Monitor*, Vol. 6, No. 56, March 24, 2009a.

———, "Ankara-Yerevan Rapprochement Strains Turkey's Relations with Azerbaijan," *Eurasia Daily Monitor*, Vol. 6, No. 68, April 9, 2009b.

———, "Acting PKK Leader Murat Karayilan Offers Rare Interview to Turkish Press," *Eurasia Daily Monitor*, Vol. 6, No. 88, May 7, 2009c.

————, "Erdogan Reassures Azerbaijan on Turkey's Border Policy with Armenia," *Eurasia Daily Monitor*, Vol. 6, No. 93, May 14, 2009d.

"U-Turn in AKP's Kurdish Policy," *Hürriyet Daily News and Economic Review* (Istanbul), November 10, 2008.

"We're Not in Any Rush to Join the EU," *Spiegel Online*, October 20, 2008. As of June 22, 2009:
http://wissen.spiegel.de/wissen/dokument/dokument.html?titel='We're+Not+in+Any+Rush+to+Join+the+EU'&id=61413102&top=SPIEGEL&suchbegriff=Muslime&quellen=

Williams, Timothy, and Suadad Al-Salhy, "Clouds Gathering over Kirkuk," *International Herald Tribune*, May 29, 2009.

Woodward, Bob, *Plan of Attack*, New York: Simon & Schuster, 2004.

Yavuz, Hakan, "Cleansing Islam from the Public Sphere," *Journal of International Affairs*, Vol. 54, No. 1, Fall 2000.

Yılmaz, Kamil, "The Emergence and Rise of Conservative Elite in Turkey," *Insight Turkey*, Vol. 11, No. 2, April–June 2009.

Yinanc, Barçin, "Outreach to Armenia Prompts Azeri Threat," *Hürriyet Daily News and Economic Review* (Istanbul), April 2, 2009.

Zaman, Amberin, "As Turkey and Armenia Inch Toward Reconciliation Both Sides Talk the Talk, But Can They Walk the Walk?" *On Turkey*, German Marshall Fund of the United States, October 2, 2008a.

————, "Turkey and the United States Under Barack Obama: Yes They Can," *On Turkey*, German Marshall Fund of the United States, November 13, 2008b.

————, "Turkey and Obama: A Golden Age in Turkish U.S. Ties," *On Turkey*, German Marshall Fund of the United States, March 20, 2009a.

————, "Turkey and Armenia," *On Turkey*, Washington, D.C.: German Marshall Fund of the United States, April 17, 2009b.

————, "Receding Power of the Military: A Leap for Democracy or Another Power Struggle?" *On Turkey*, German Marshall Fund of the United States, July 15, 2009c.

————, "Turkey's Kurds: Toward a Solution," *On Turkey*, German Marshall Fund of the United States, June 4, 2009d.